A JOURNEY THROUGH
THE SCOTTISH BORDERS

JIM COLLINS

FRONT AND BACK COVER: **RIVER TWEED NEAR MERTOUN**

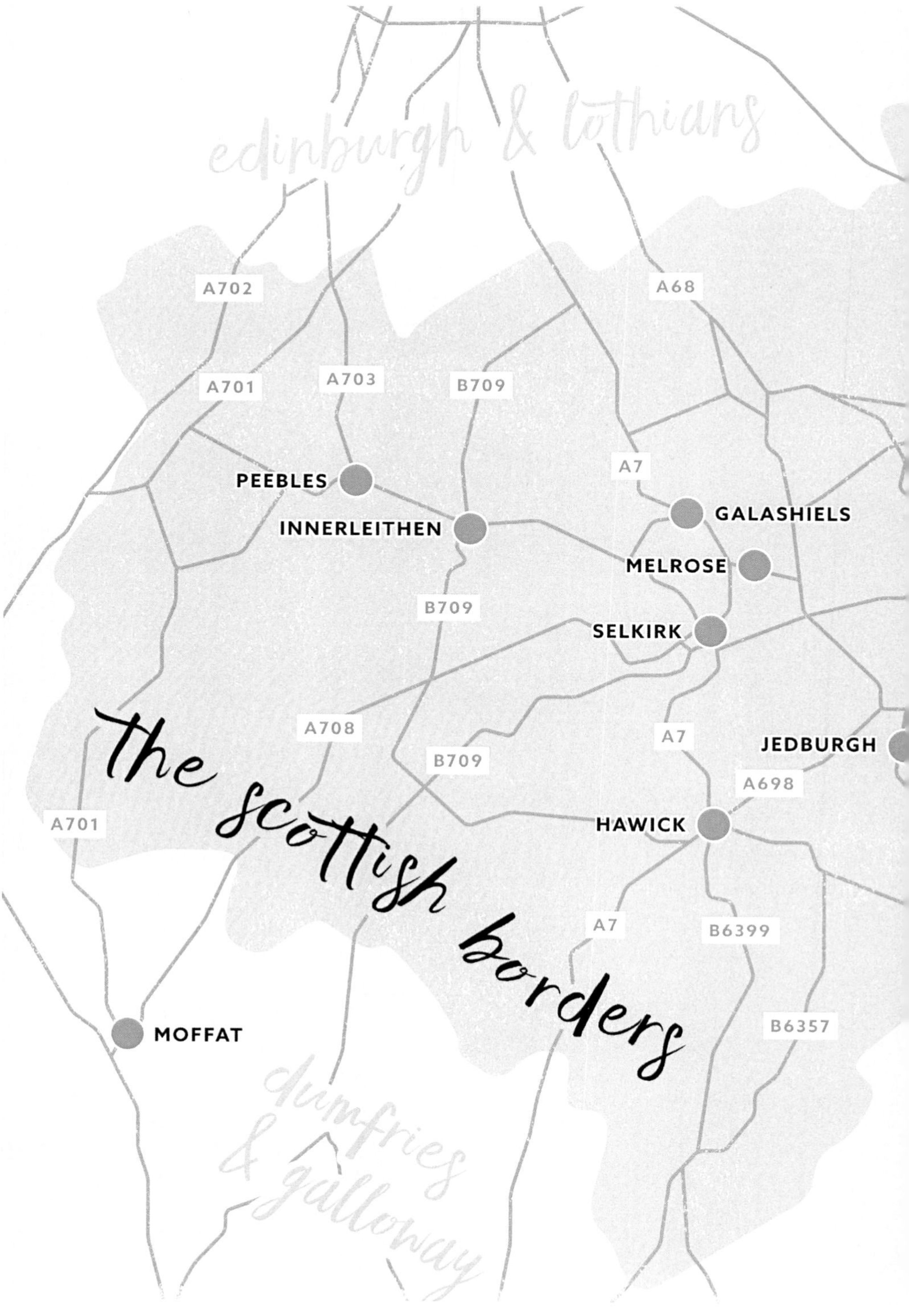
edinburgh & lothians
A702
A68
A701
A703
B709
A7
PEEBLES
GALASHIELS
INNERLEITHEN
MELROSE
B709
SELKIRK
A708
A7
JEDBURGH
B709
A698
A701
HAWICK
A7
B6399
B6357
MOFFAT
the scottish borders
dumfries & galloway

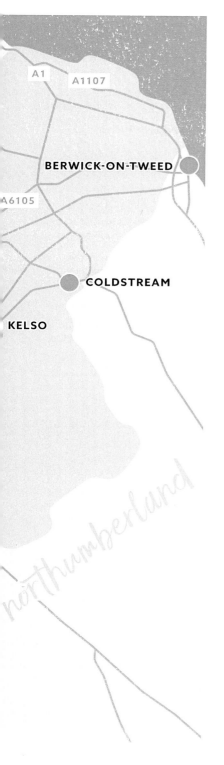

CONTENTS

introduction

When I first had the idea of putting pen to paper and writing a few words about the Scottish Borders, it was my intention only to feature the towns of Melrose, Galashiels and Selkirk. These were the three main towns adjacent to the area in which I had lived and spent my childhood years. These towns particularly Melrose and Galashiels were the centres of my educational and social needs as a youngster and held many memories. My writings were going to be in the form of an essay, (remember them from school days?) and therefore, it was never going to be more than a few paragraphs long. This at least is what I initially thought. The thinking behind it all was to have a written record of my childhood memories before they disappeared and became obscured in the mists and fog of old age. It was going to be something purely for my own personal satisfaction, something that perhaps my grandchildren could read in years to come, it might even be possible for my musings to be spotted and recognized for their literary genius and added to a tourist magazine as a page filler.

It was only when I started to do some initial research however, to try and expand the few thoughts I had, that it became clear that there was considerably more that I could and should write about this particular area of Scotland. There was certainly more to be told than could be summarized in just a few short paragraphs, that was becoming very evident. A further revelation from doing this initial research was that the one common factor linking all my thoughts and memories was the River Tweed. An idea then began to take shape in my mind, that the Tweed, being very much a part of the Scottish Borders, should be the basis for a more detailed story, which could then be developed to include the towns, the villages, the grand country houses, the vast estates which are either situated on or very close to its banks and the history which is deeply imbedded throughout the region with each of these parts having its own story to tell.

What follows therefore are my thoughts and impressions, my insight, and a few of the tales that emerged, some very surprising, as I followed the River Tweed downstream from its source, on the Western side of Scotland to its point of entry into the North sea at Berwick-on-Tweed on the East Coast near the Scottish Border. During the course of my travels, I knew, if nothing else, there would always be the idyllic countryside, which changes with every bend of the river. There is the history surrounding Scotland's greatest salmon river, tales from the towns and villages which for the most part border its banks and the realization that the river was and still is, a major contributor not only to the Borders economy and lifestyle, but also indeed to Scotland's economy as a whole. There are also places which are visited and discussed which, whilst not necessarily that close to the Tweed are mentioned purely and simply because of their importance in Borders history and culture, consequently they could not be excluded from a story relating to this area. In fact so much of interest was uncovered during the research stages that it was very difficult to decide what should and should not be included, (A hint of a second book perhaps?) What follows is by no means meant to be a definitive guide to the Borders or indeed a detailed history, instead I hope that if you are reading this, it will perhaps create an interest and an inner desire to visit not only the places I mention but the surrounding areas as well. To my mind, even taking into account my undeniable love of the area, the Scottish Borders are a hidden gem waiting to be discovered and explored.

RIVER TWEED NEAR ABBOTSFORD

CHAPTER 1

If you look at a map of the British Isles, about half way up on the left hand side lies the City of Carlisle and just to the north of Carlisle sits the village of Gretna, this is where the Scottish English Border starts. From here it snakes its way following the contours of the land North and East through Northumberland and the Cheviot Hills until it reaches Berwick-Upon-Tweed. Having a picture in your mind of how the Border is situated in relation to the places we will be passing through will help you to understand how this area was in a virtual constant state of conflict for hundreds of years. We begin our journey however and the stories connected with it, in the picturesque town of Moffat. Situated just over forty miles north of Carlisle, Moffat itself is well worth a visit and very popular with tourists and day-trippers alike. Why begin our tale in Moffat? The source of the River Tweed is less than six miles from Moffat and as a place to have an overnight stay, to gather information, and to make plans and preparations for the trip ahead, it makes an ideal starting point.

Moffat, as well as being a handy stop over point for travellers heading either North or South, was also well known throughout the United Kingdom for it spa and hot water curative treatments. The town had been providing spa facilities from as early as 1827. The sulphorous waters were reputed to have healing properties and were piped from the

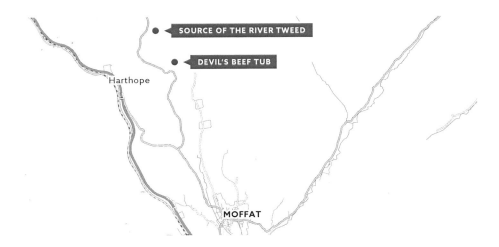

SOURCE OF THE RIVER TWEED

DEVIL'S BEEF TUB

Harthope

MOFFAT

hillsides over a mile away from the town to a public bath house in the town centre, where both visitors and local residents alike could either drink or bathe in the heated waters. The late 18th century and early 19th centuries were when the Spa was at its height of popularity and Moffat was alive with visitors who had come to "take the cure". Many hotels were built in the town to satisfy the needs of the people visiting the Spa and one of those hotels, The Star Hotel located in the market square is mentioned in the Guinness Book of Records as being the narrowest hotel in the world. At just twenty feet or six metres wide, it certainly has all the necessary credentials to lay claim to that particular record.

Moffat was also one of the recognized centres and markets for the wool and sheep trades, a flourishing industry during the 1800's in the Borders. This fact is commemorated by a statue, in the town centre, by Scottish sculptor William Brodie, of a ram, which from its perch on a rocky outcrop surveys the market place. An unusual feature of this statue is that the ram's ears are missing, which apparently when pointed out by a local farmer during the grand unveiling ceremony, caused the sculptor a certain amount of embarrassment. There is a suggestion locally, totally unsubstantiated, I must add, that this troubled William Brodie, so much that it in fact led to his death and his ghost wanders the corridors of a nearby hotel searching for the missing "lugs" (Scottish word for ears) of that poor unfortunate ram.

First time visitors to Moffat are advised to be cautious as the traffic passing through the town centre, travels in either direction on both sides of the town square and many an unwary pedestrian has had to be reminded of this by a gentle "toot" from a car horn. This little local anomaly is more than compensated for however by the range of shops available to browse around. There are a number of very interesting independent shops in and around the centre of Moffat. The oldest pharmacy in Scotland is here, with some of the original shop fittings still intact. There is also an old fashioned confectioners and sweet shop, where the sweets, which were undoubtedly part of your childhood and which you probably thought had gone out of production years and years ago are there on the shelves, displayed in those great big glass jars, (although they are more likely to be made from perspex these days.) By way of contrast to these two older style shops, situated on a narrow street radiating out from the square is a delicatessen which has a cold counter packed with meats and cheeses, shelves brimming with jars and tins of every conceivable delicacy and piles of bread not only baked the old fashioned way but tasting the way that perhaps your parents or grandparents can remember. After perusing the contents of this shop you may very well feel hunger pangs yourself and if this is the case there are at various points around the market square in Moffat a variety of cafes and restaurants all within easy walking distance which will be able to satisfy your inner desires should that be required. Moffat is a very accessible town, being positioned just off the M74 motorway and is approximately less than sixty miles from both Edinburgh and Glasgow. In fact if the Median Centre by Latitude and Longitude method of calculation is used, one mile North of Moffat is the exact Centre of Britain.

Inspector Jeremiah Lynch from Scotland Yard was one of the detectives involved in the case and he had available to him what was then a relatively new detection system, but which is now known as Forensics. After examining the evidence collected thus far, it was decided that Doctor Ruxton should again be visited by the police to clear up a few points and this time his house was extensively searched. Finger print samples were collected from the house and during the search several small blood spots were discovered. Doctor Ruxton explained them away by saying they were from a cut on his hand. One part of this new detection system which the police were able to use was the facility to overlay an x-ray picture of a skull over a suspected victims photograph and when this was done in this particular case, Inspector Lynch was informed that there was an exact likeness to one of the skulls discovered in Moffat. This and the various other samples collected from the house meant the police were able to identify the two bodies found in Moffat as being Mrs. Isabella Ruxton the doctor's wife and Mary Jane Rogerson their cleaner and children's nanny.

It would appear that the "good" doctor had become increasingly jealous of his wife's popularity as she played her part in the local social scene in the area where he practiced. This jealousy had finally reached the point of no return and after an argument with his wife regarding an alleged affair, he snapped and on the 15th September 1935 strangled her. In order to prevent their cleaner from discovering the body before he could dispose of it, or perhaps because she had witnessed Doctor Ruxton actually committing the crime, he took the decision to murder her as well. Doctor Ruxton had earlier in his career trained to be a surgeon but failed his final exams and never qualified. He now used the skills he had learned whilst training to be a surgeon to mutilate and dismember the two bodies in the bath at his house. He was familiar with the Moffat countryside having passed through it on several occasions whilst traveling to and from Edinburgh. He therefore decided to dispose of the bodies in what he considered would be a place where they would not be discovered. His devious plan and medical expertise however, was no match for the new detection systems and the diligence of the police officers involved in the case. He was arrested and charged in October 1935 with the murders. His trial lasted for eleven days. There was a tremendous amount of evidence against him and the jury found him guilty and he was sentenced to death. Surprisingly, despite the horrific nature of the crime he had committed, a petition calling for clemency on behalf of the doctor had nearly ten thousand signatures. The petition however was denied and the death sentence was carried out in May 1936 when he was hanged at Strangeways Prison in Manchester. For many years after being hanged Doctor Ruxton's waxwork effigy was on display at Madame Tussauds House of Horrors in London.

With Moffat's past, both good and bad, behind us, we will begin our journey of exploration by heading away from Moffat on the main A701 road towards Edinburgh. We travel along this road admiring the Borders scenery for approximately six miles to where the real story begins.

CHAPTER 2

the source, romans, stobo castle, dawyck arboretum

The source of the River Tweed is generally recognized as being Tweed's Well an open area of heathland situated in the Lowther Hills, these hills form the Western side of the Southern Uplands which lie just North of the town of Moffat, in the Southerly part of the county of Peebles. As is so often the case with the origins of rivers, there is a slight disagreement from a number of people who say the real source of the Tweed is in fact another spring which has its beginnings only a quarter of a mile away, but as this other spring actually joins up with the Tweed less than fifty yards from its Tweed's Well source, it is of no great consequence other than to the purists. In fact the point marking the source of the Tweed was to my mind anyway, perhaps a little underwhelming, I am not quite sure what I was expecting to see, so perhaps the image in my mind as I travelled along the road from Moffat, of a massed pipe band, with dancers in traditional Scottish dress, performing reels and strathspeys, for visitors looking for the source, was probably too much to hope for. In reality I suppose even a river as grand as the Tweed, has to start somewhere and that starting point inevitably is on rather a small scale. Only a sign and a large stone block in a lay-by at the side of the road, informs those who care to stop and read the inscriptions on it, that the source of the Tweed in fact starts on the opposite side of the road, in a vast expanse of open moorland

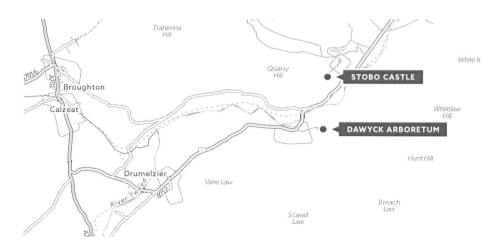

which unfortunately is fenced off and not open to the public. Apart from admiring what is a particularly pleasant view from the side of the road there is very little else to see.

It doesn't take very long however from this point, for the myriad of small brooks and rivulets which drain from the surrounding hillsides to merge into what becomes a sizeable stream and at last the River Tweed starts to take shape. The Tweed is the fourth or fifth longest river in Scotland and the tenth or eleventh longest river in the United Kingdom, depending on what source of information you use. If however you were able to travel in a straight line from its source to its emergence into the North Sea at Berwick-upon-Tweed you would cover a distance of nearly sixty five miles, (104 kilometres.) Rivers though, have a tendency not to travel in straight lines, but prefer instead to take the line of least resistance across the terrain they are running through and the Tweed is no exception. It meanders through the beautiful Borders countryside, for most of the time anyway in a rather unhurried fashion and consequently increases its overall length to approximately ninety seven miles, (155 kilometres.) For some ten miles of that distance, (16 kilometres) as it gets ever nearer to Berwick-upon-Tweed, the River Tweed forms the actual physical Border between England and Scotland and has been the backdrop for many bloody conflicts over the centuries, many of these battles will be covered in more detail during the course of our downstream journey.

The hillsides around Tweeds Well are also the beginnings of two other great Scottish rivers, the River Annan and the River Clyde, The three sources being so close resulted in an old rhyme (author unknown) which states "Annan, Tweed and Clyde Rise a' oot o' ae hill side". Which roughly translated means that these three rivers all start from the one hillside. Although all three rivers more or less start together, it is only the Tweed which flows eastwards towards the North Sea, as the Clyde flows westward towards Glasgow and the Firth of Clyde, and the Annan flows South and West towards the Solway Firth and the Irish Sea. "Firth" is generally a Scottish lowland term, which denotes the area of entry of a river into the sea. The most apt comparison would probably be to the word "Fjord" a description which is used for similar geographic features in many Scandinavian countries.

The slight confusion regarding the actual source of the Tweed is also reflected in the origin of its name, with the most generally accepted version being as follows. The countryside of the Scottish Borders, whilst it is very scenic and beautiful, was not agricultural land, especially in the days before powered machinery became available to help farmers, It was though, ideal countryside for grazing and virtually all the farms had either flocks of sheep or herds of cattle, some of the larger farms maybe even had both. These animals would roam the hills and moorland feeding on the rich grass especially during the summer months. The fleeces from these flocks of sheep were then made into a fairly rough unfinished textile product called Tweel by the many woollen mills common to the Borders region. The story is that a London merchant having received his order from Scotland which included a hand written letter and invoice, mistook the word Tweel for Tweed and marketed it as such and the name stuck. There is also another very acceptable alternative theory as to how the river may have got its name and this is it. Water from the river was one of the main sources of power available in the early days of textile production and part of the flow of the Tweed was diverted using mill lades and sluices (small canals and gates). This current of water was then used via water wheels to power the machinery in these mills. The water not only washed the fleeces but provided the necessary power for machines to turn the fleeces into this textile product which had become known as Tweed, therefore it has been suggested that the river was named after the product it produced. Regardless of which of these stories is true, the name Tweed has remained and is known throughout the world. During the course of our travels downstream there will be many references to woollen mills and you will see the importance that the woollen trade had, not only for the local economies of the various Border towns, but also Scotland's national economy as well.

The Romans played a significant part in the early history of Scotland and this particular area of Scotland has many connections with the Roman Empire. There are what is known as marching forts, the remains of which are visible either side of Peebles, one of the largest Border towns at which we will be arriving very soon. These marching forts were basically the motorway service stations of their day and were used not only as overnight stops for troops when they were involved in campaigns but also as barracks to house a small contingent of troops to protect the roads the Romans had built during their occupation. These were used as a quick means of transport for troops and equipment in their battles against the "Britunculli" as they were known to the Roman soldiers, this was a rather derogatory description of the clansmen in this area and loosely translated meant "Wretched Britons."

There is also a certain amount of speculation regarding a Roman Legion which effectively "disappeared" from all recorded history. This legion was the famous Ninth legion, about which many articles and books have been researched and written in an attempt to find out what actually happened to them. There have even been films made, two in particular "Centurion" and "Eagle of the Ninth" have attempted to discover the truth about what happened and why recorded history of the "Ninth" just stopped without any explanation. At this period in history, the Romans were invincible, they were well trained, well fed, well armed and well organized. They had already conquered and were in control of vast areas of the then known world before they even landed and invaded what was to become known as Britain. It would therefore be unthinkable to the populace of Rome that such a highly trained, efficient and experienced army could suffer defeat at the hands of what was generally regarded as barbarian hordes. This however is one of the theories put forward as to the fate of the Ninth legion.

If in fact the Ninth Legion had come to such a sticky end it would have been the policy of the Roman Empire not to let defeats, especially of this magnitude be revealed to the civilian population at home in Rome and as such it would have been covered up. This policy of covering up bad news was possibly why all records and information relating to the Ninth Legion, seem to have disappeared. It has been suggested that this particular part of Scotland is one possible site where such a catastrophic defeat could have taken place, as the Ninth Legion had been sent here to deal with tribal unrest shortly before all records concerning them ceased. An alternative theory that has been put forward as to what happened to the missing legion is that after campaigning in Scotland they were transferred to another theatre of war in Europe. Certainly a feasible explanation but it still does not however explain the complete absence of any records. Therefore with no substantial evidence either way I am tempted, as a patriotic Scotsman to believe the former story and accept that against all the odds the Ninth Legion were completely vanquished by a rag tag mix of tribesmen from this area and beyond.

One encounter that is fairly well documented is the Battle of Mons Graupius (Grampian Mountains). The story relating to this battle and the one which was told to the citizens of Rome, is that having suffered continual attacks and ambushes from the "Britunculli" the Romans had decided that enough was enough and had deployed an army of considerable strength to show these Northern Tribes just who was in control. The local individual tribes had realized from earlier battles that there was in fact strength in numbers and they had come together and were now a united force. They were even using some of the battle tactics which had been deployed against them to great effect by the Romans themselves in previous encounters and the clans and tribesmen were now a real threat to Roman dominance. The actual site of the Battle of Mons Graupius has never been discovered, there are even some historians who believe it may never even have taken place at all and that it is only one of those stories that gets bigger and better the more it is told. The reports however of this battle which arrived back in Rome, were dictated by Tacitus, a well respected historian and the details he recounted to the inhabitants of Rome spoke of a thirty thousand plus force of barbarians being wiped out by a Roman army of half that number, as mentioned earlier though, only good news concerning campaigns was relayed back to Rome, so was this story of such a convincing victory, just an attempt to compensate for the dramatic and drastic loss of the Ninth Legion? Bearing in mind that a Legion of that period consisted of approximately five thousand men, with possibly a cavalry troop of more than a hundred men and horses attached to it, plus of course all the people that traveled with such a large force in order to keep them functioning on a day to day basis. Therefore it is difficult to imagine that the Roman Command could have disbanded or moved to another area or another country such a large body of troops without somebody noticing or making a written comment. Once again, therefore the story of a complete annihilation begins to be more believable. Despite there being no proof of a battle or even a battle site, relics from this and many other periods of history do turn up from time to time, the truth may very well be lying somewhere just under the surface of a Border field, waiting to be unearthed, either by a farmer ploughing his fields, or perhaps a lucky amateur hoping to discover buried treasure using a metal detector.

The turbulent history of The Borders resulted in many fine castles, keeps and watchtowers being built, a number of which are still in existence and indeed still lived in today. The first of these as we travel downriver from Tweed's Well is Stobo Castle. The construction of Stobo Castle as it is now, began in the early 1800's although there had been a building of sorts there for nearly forty years before that. Various people and families have laid claim to Stobo Castle and each has had their own part in re-designing and extending not only the actual building but also the grounds and gardens. Stobo Castle's most recent purchase has seen the castle transformed into a Luxury Health and Beauty Spa, in conjunction with a five star hotel, one of the few ways these days that buildings of this size and their grounds can be maintained and their history preserved.

Only a matter of a few minutes from Stobo Castle by road, is Dawyck Botanic Gardens, listed as a World Class Arboretum. Scotland, and the United Kingdom generally has surprisingly, very few native tree species. One variety which because it is so common in the U.K. would automatically lead anybody to think of it as being a native species, is in fact reputed to have been introduced to these shores by the Romans and that tree is the Horse Chestnut. The climate in Scotland and this area in particular is conducive to growing trees and because of this, seeds and specimens were collected and brought here from all over the world by various explorers and plant hunters including Thomas Drummond, Archibald Menzies (Monkey Puzzle tree) David Douglas after whom the Douglas Fir is named, and many others who brought specimens back from their travels round the globe. Dawyck Arboretum now covers nearly sixty five acres of Scottish hillside which not only contains some of the biggest, oldest and tallest trees in Britain but also has a huge variety of plants and shrubs gathered from all over the world which are growing quite happily here in Scotland. Dawyck prides itself on being able to provide a different viewing experience no matter what time of year you visit. There are huge displays of snowdrops and daffodils in the early spring, followed by the spectacular colours of massed plantings of rhododendrons, azaleas, and blue Himalayan poppies sourced from Nepal, China and Chile. This in turn is followed by the striking autumnal colours of gold, orange and various shades of red with fruits and berries on many trees and shrubs. All year round, the different shades of green from the vast collection of conifers from every corner of the world contrast with the ever changing colours of the deciduous trees and the various species of shrubs planted across the hillside.

DAWYCK ARBORETUM

DAWYCK ARBORETUM

There are designated pathways to follow with information boards, signs and quite often labels on the trees giving details of size, variety and country of origin. There is also a special area, the Cryptogamic Sanctuary, and no don't worry, I didn't know what it was, or meant either, but apparently it is a special reserve for lichens, fungi, mosses and liverworts, which play a very important part in maintaining a healthy balance in any wild woodland botanical area. Dawyck is open to the public from the 1st of February right through until the end of November, which leaves only two months of the year when the woodlands are free of visitors for the workers employed at the Arboretum to attend to a lot of the jobs which cannot be done when there are crowds of people strolling through the woods. Dawyck also features an award winning visitor centre which contains a restaurant serving everything from a snack to a light meal, with an open air sitting area available in which you can enjoy your meal during the summer months. A separate studio is also available for special events and exhibitions. There is, as always the inevitable shop at the visitor centre which as well as stocking a large range of gift items also has a selection of plants most of which reflect local varieties and are grown in the vicinity as well.

We leave Dawyck and re-join the main road, continuing for another eight miles (13 kilometres) to our next stop.

ROAD BRIDGE CROSSING RIVER TWEED AT PEEBLES

peebles, neidpath castle and viaduct, kailzie gardens, glentress

The first major town through which the River Tweed flows is Peebles, twenty six miles (42 kilometres) from its source. In that distance the River Tweed has dropped seven hundred feet below its starting point height. Given that its total drop throughout its entire length is less than thirteen hundred feet it means that the remaining seventy miles or so of the river provides long stretches of relatively calm water with deep pools and a steady flow of water interspersed with bubbling rapids which help to provide the highly oxygenated water necessary for fish and plant life to survive. These conditions have resulted in the River Tweed gaining the well deserved reputation for being not only the best salmon fishing river in Scotland but also one of the best in the world. Peebles has its fair share of excellent fishing "beats", (a "beat" is the name given to a specific stretch of river) and the best time of year for salmon fishing in the Peebles area is late Summer and Autumn. Haystoun Beat is located just downstream from Peebles itself and consists of seven named pools including "Kerfield" "Blackthroat" and "Wirebridge" It is in these pools that salmon are likely to be resting and recuperating after having battled their way upstream, a journey which may well have taken them several weeks. Salmon of course are not the only fish available to anglers in the Borders area, there are also trout, sea trout, and grayling. These varieties of fish are

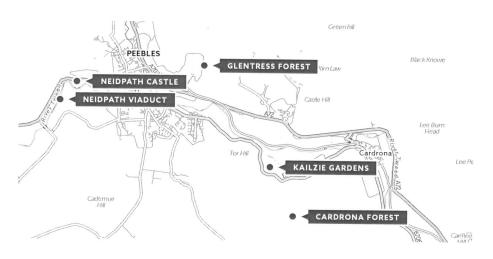

NEIDPATH CASTLE

NEIDPATH VIADUCT

the incidents mentioned in the previous pages and is now the third biggest town in the Borders with a thriving population, helped by the fact that it is only twenty three miles (37 kilometres) from Edinburgh, Scotland's capital city. Peebles and district therefore are now regarded as very much part of the commuter belt. The beauty of living in this region if you are a commuting worker, is that the problems and cares of the working week can be left behind when you arrive home, as you have not only the beautiful scenery but all the benefits and attractions of the countryside right on your doorstep.

What Peebles has managed to avoid, thankfully, despite its big population increase, is the scourge of many modern towns and cities and that is having a High Street filled with retail premises owned by national chains. Both residents and visitors alike are able to shop and enjoy products and produce from small, independent, local suppliers. To give you an idea of the diversity of business interests you can find in Peebles, here are two examples of what is available. There is a business, owned by a gentleman called Martin Swan, who is a professional violinist and specializes in selling antique violins and bows, however he also makes violins, violas and cellos using professional craftsmen, to meet the specific needs of each individual client. He also gives personal advice and service to any of his customers who are looking to fulfill their musical dreams. If this particular venture can be regarded as being one end of the spectrum we then go to the other end, where we find Cocoa Black, from the outside, it is a café, but inside are the most fabulous home made cakes, chocolates and patisserie items you could possibly imagine. If just eating these mouth watering goodies whilst enjoying a cup of coffee is not enough for you, Cocoa Black also hosts various courses

KAILZIE GARDENS

designed to help you make and perfect your own creations. There is quite a difference as you can appreciate between these two enterprises, but that is what life in the Borders can be like.

Scotland has produced many literary greats and in that list John Buchan must rank very high. He is perhaps most well known for his book "The Thirty Nine Steps" of which there have also been various film adaptations. However there is considerably more to his writings than just that one book, he was a prolific writer, not only of books, but numerous magazine articles and stories as well. He was also a politician, civil servant, journalist, novelist, historian and soldier. In 1935 he was appointed Governor General of Canada, he became a Baron and took the name Lord Tweedsmuir of Elsfield. The John Buchan museum was formerly at Broughton, a village only a short distance from Peebles but the museum has been moved and re-located in early 2013 to Peebles High Street where it was felt that more visitors to the region would be able to see and learn about everything John Buchan had achieved in his life.

There are quite a number of attractions very close to Peebles one of these is Kailzie Gardens, only two and a half miles (4 kilometres) from Peebles and consisting not only of gardens and various walks, but fishing tuition, with several ponds containing trout in which to test your newly acquired skills. There is also an Osprey watching site which has three cameras capturing real time pictures from the Osprey's nest. Similarly there are also cameras watching a Heron's nest which at the time of my visit had three eggs in it. There is usually at least one volunteer at the viewing station, able to answer any questions you may have, regarding the various projects that they are undertaking at any one time. There are also many woodland and garden walks, a putting green, walled garden, and a children's play area, plus various specialized areas which feature hundreds if not thousands of plants which provide all year round colour and interest. You can easily spend an inordinate amount of time exploring the grounds and looking at the other attractions, so Kailzie has very thoughtfully included a restaurant in the main block which provides everything from a cup of tea or coffee to a full blown meal. Because of the scenic nature of the gardens and grounds Kailzie has become a very popular venue for weddings, so don't be surprised if you suddenly find yourself in the midst of a bridal party. What makes these gardens extra special though is that they are positioned over seven hundred feet above sea level on the south bank of the River Tweed which means the cultivated area mainly faces North and East a daunting prospect for any prospective gardener. If that is not enough of a problem also throw into the mix the fact that frosts have been recorded here during every month of the year. Frosts during the winter months have been known to be sometimes as low as minus twenty degrees Centigrade, a frost of twelve degrees was even recorded one midsummer's day!! Plants therefore have to be fairly hardy to survive, but for the most part it is the work of the dedicated gardeners employed here, who have proved beyond doubt that with determination and perseverance and of course the right plants, a beautiful garden can be created, even under the unlikeliest of conditions.

KAILZIE GARDENS

Less than a mile and a half (2.5 kilometres) to the East of Peebles lies Glentress Forest. Perhaps like me you may have heard the name but never realized its significance, if that is the case you are probably not a fan or an exponent of mountain biking. Glentress Forest is regarded as the Mecca of mountain biking. The Forestry Commision Scotland have invested considerable sums of money over the last few years into this project and it has paid off handsomely. There are various routes available, colour coded to denote difficulty from green which is classed as easy through to blue which is moderate, red difficult and black which is classed as severe and the lengths of the routes vary from three and a half kilometres (approx. two miles) to a muscle aching twenty nine kilometres (approx. eighteen miles) There are trails at Glentress which are designed specifically for beginners, families and children, there are also practice and free ride areas as well, so all in all there is something for everybody regardless of what skill level you are at, or what you would like to achieve. To give you an idea of what to expect, there is the eighteen kilometre Red route. This is favoured by the majority of the biking fraternity and the descent into Spooky Wood I am told is regarded as being one of the best fun factors around.

If however you are not content with the Red route and want to test your skills even further, then there is also the awesome Black route, twenty nine kilometres (eighteen miles) of everything that mountain bikers could possibly want. It is not as you may have deduced, a trail for novices or indeed the faint hearted. It has I have been told, been completed in something like an hour and a half by super fit professionals, but "normal" human beings are expected to finish the course in something between three and five hours. With uphill climb sections of the route known as "Redemption" and "Deliverance" and downhill sections named "The Bitch" and "The Worm Hole" which are described on the website as "tricky" I shall leave it up to you which routes you would prefer to tackle. As you would expect from such a popular facility as this, there is everything you could possibly need on site, from bike hire, spares and repairs to showers for riders and washing facilities for the bikes as well. Plus of course the all important food and drink to replenish all that energy which has been used up racing through the forest. There are several websites which can give you considerably more detail about the condition of the trails, weather, plus the services and facilities on offer at Glentress, so if mountain biking and trail riding are your hearts desire it's well worth spending a few minutes checking what is available, especially during holidays and busy periods, you won't be disappointed.

One of the many good things which is evident during an exploration of the Tweed Valley is the fact that everything is relatively close at hand wherever you are. If you are travelling by car, the road, or at least a road of some description, not necessarily the main road, is close at hand and this also applies to walking trails and cycling routes as well. Even the towns and villages are within easy reach of each other and therefore sustenance either in a liquid or solid form and indeed accommodation if it is required, is never too far away. The River Tweed is never going to match the romantic ideals of the Seine, the rugged adventures associated with navigating the Amazon, or the cruise capabilities of the Nile but the towns and villages, the history, the scenery, the wildlife and the people that live close to its banks with the stories they have to tell give the Tweed its own special significance and charm. I hope that as you delve deeper into these pages, it will perhaps awaken an interest inside you and create a desire to come and see all the things that I mention and possibly discover even more Border treasures for yourselves.

Just under seven miles from Kailzie gardens and Peebles, lies Cardrona Forest and the town of Innerleithen. Cardrona has forest walks, a wildlife centre, cycling and horse riding trails. If golf is your particular fancy then there is an eighteen hole championship course close by with a four star hotel and spa complex alongside.

If you are perhaps looking for something a little out of the ordinary, especially when it boils down to trying to keep young children amused then maybe the Velvet Hall Alpacas would be the answer. These animals will accompany you on walks and treks over the local hills, seemingly very glad of the human company and very friendly towards children and indeed adults as well. Walks and treks can be tailored to meet your particular needs and requirements, or you can just meet the Alpacas and pet them at the centre. It is suggested though that because of the centre's popularity, particularly during the summer months that you contact them first before visiting. Just enter Velvet Hall Alpacas into whatever search option you have and you will then be able to find all the information you need regarding opening hours and availability etc.

CHAPTER 4

innerleithen, traquair, walkerburn, clovenfords, ashiestiel, salmon

Innerleithen, whilst being in the top ten largest Border settlements is still able to maintain a village atmosphere and has amongst its attractions, St Ronan's Wells, a former spa which still sells bottled water obtained from the deep underground sources which made it famous all these years ago. Don't forget to also visit Robert Smail's print shop now owned by The National Trust for Scotland but which dates back to 1866 with most of the original machinery and equipment still in place. Why not pay a visit to the shop and learn how to type-set your own piece of printing? Both Innerleithen and Glentress (mentioned in the previous chapter) biking centres are part of the "7 Stanes Group" which is basically seven mountain biking centres spread across the South of Scotland. "Stane" is the Scottish word for stone and each centre has a stone sculpture created by the award winning artist Gordon Young. He has in his sculptures taken a local story or a legend connected to the area and reflected that theme within the sculpture, some of Gordon's sculptures at these featured sites can be up to ten feet tall and weigh in the region of six tons, a very impressive sight as you cycle round the trails. Innerleithen like Glentress also has several different levels of trail difficulty but it is probably best known for its "Extreme" downhill trails, which are recognized as being amongst the best, if not the best, in Scotland and possibly the U.K. In

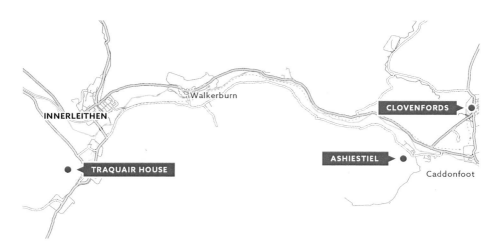

fact these trails are regularly used in both Scottish and British rounds of the Downhill Series as well as the increasingly popular "Winter Race Series" The runs are designed as far as I can understand more for serious bikers than for family outings, but for more up to date information, please once again check out the local websites, to get all the details you need regarding opening times, condition of the trails and prices.

The river Leithen from which Innerleithen gets its name, is one of the many tributaries of the Tweed and in the days when wool was king had part of its flow diverted via a mill lade to provide both the power and the water required to wash the sheep fleeces for up to five woollen mills in the town. (Sustainable power is not an idea that has only been thought of in the 21stCentury.) The force of the water also powered a water wheel at a sawmill positioned just before the Mill lade and the River Leithen rejoins the River Tweed to continue its eastward journey. Unfortunately, the sawmill is no longer operating and the last textile mill in Innerleithen which had been in operation for over two hundred and twenty years, employing more than four hundred people at its peak, finally closed its doors in April this year (2013.)

Less than two miles (four kilometres) downstream from Innerleithen lies Traquair House which has the proud boast of being the oldest inhabited house in Scotland. The Quair burn, another stream which feeds into the Tweed and the old Celtic word "Tre" make up the name Traquair which basically means a dwelling place by a winding stream. Traquair or at least a house of some considerable size had been in existence on this site since the very early 12th Century. It was used as a hunting lodge for Royals and nobility who hunted in the nearby forest for amongst other things deer, bear, wolves and wild boar. The late 13th Century was a time of conflict and strife and Traquair House was a frequent target for

TRAQUAIR HOUSE

THE MAIZE AT TRAQUAIR HOUSE

attacks. Traquair and their neighbours had in place an early warning system which consisted of a beacon located at the highest point of the house. If an attack was imminent or indeed taking place a fire was lit and thus neighbours were alerted to danger by either the smoke from the fire during the day or by the flames from the fire at night. They in turn lit their fires to warn their neighbours of trouble which in that period was mainly caused by the English, and indeed at one point Traquair was occupied, but only very briefly, by English troops.

The house has had a number of owners, but in 1491 came under the ownership of James Stewart the first Laird (Lord) of Traquair and has remained in that family to this day. Many troubles be-fell the owners of Traquair during the 18th Century due mainly to their staunch Catholic and Jacobite beliefs. The seventh Earl's love of gambling, and several failed business ventures didn't help the situation either. Because of these problems, maintenance issues had been overlooked and Traquair House was badly in need of love and attention.

It wasn't until after the Second World War when government grants became available to restore the great historic houses of Britain that Traquair began to re-emerge and in 1953 the house was first opened to the public but on a very limited basis. Ten years later in 1963 it had become evident that a house of this size needed a much larger income just to cover the costs of repairs and maintenance. By this time the house was owned by Peter Maxwell Stuart the 20th Laird of Traquair and his wife Flora and it was during his ownership that Traquair was developed into a major tourist attraction including the re-instating of the old domestic brewery in 1965. The brewery had not been in use for nearly two hundred years and it was a major as well as a costly exercise putting everything back into working order.

The good side of all this effort meant that the famous Traquair ales which had been brewed there when the brewery was first in existence, were re-born, two of the most well known being the award winning Traquair Ale and Bear Ale. Sadly Peter Maxwell died in 1990 and Traquair was inherited by his wife and daughter and they continued to run it for the next decade adding all the time to the attractions available, which now include weddings, bed and breakfast rooms, and a range of featured events particularly during the summer months. In 1999 Flora re-married and retired from running Traquair house, leaving it to her daughter Catherine the twenty first Lady of Traquair and a charitable trust. Catherine her husband and three children still live in and use the house as their family home.

Walkerburn the next village we arrive at on our journey along the banks of the River Tweed is literally just a few minutes South of Innerleithen. Its name comes from the Walker burn which runs through the village and joins the Tweed. This burn (Scottish word for small stream) was again the principal supply of water for use in the woollen mills around which Walkerburn was built. This township came about because of the vision of one man, Henry Ballantyne, who had several woollen mills in the area and he had been considering for some time the idea of providing people with not only a job but housing as well. In his mind was the fact that in order for him to expand his tweed mills he would need more workers. The current situation was that he was having more and more to tempt workers to work in his mills from farther and farther away. The travelling involved in getting to and from work added considerably to their time away from their homes and family, and in winter especially, heavy snowfalls could mean that he didn't have any workforce at all. If he was able to provide housing, next to or very close to the factory, they would be able to work longer hours for him, producing considerably more goods and thereby increasing his profits. As the houses "given" to the workers were part of their wages, they would have to continue working for him to keep a roof over their heads and so, apart from the initial cost of building the houses, there was little further expense involved for Mr. Ballantyne. His tweed mill in Walkerburn was built in 1846 and he then began to build houses for his workers and so the village was born. It was completed by 1854 and such was the importance of the woollen trade to the area that by 1866 Walkerburn even had its own railway line, with daily services offering direct links to Scotland's capital city, Edinburgh. The railway was the ideal solution for taking the finished product from the mills to the wider markets in the capital, as well as being an alternative supply route to bring raw materials to the mills. With Edinburgh's rail link to London, the potential market for Tweed and the other textile products they produced was huge not only throughout the U.K. but the wider world as well. This was the golden age for tweed and textiles, but sadly, as is so often the case due to ever increasing competition from both home and abroad neither the woollen mills nor the railway line still exist. Walkerburn, whilst it is still a very picturesque village to visit, now houses only memories of that by-gone era in the shape of The Museum of Scottish Textiles.

Having lived in the Borders for at least fifteen years, a period which covered both my primary and secondary school education, I considered myself to be fairly knowledgeable and well acquainted with the area that I had grown up in. Therefore it was with a great deal of surprise that during the course of my journey down the Tweed and the Tweed Valley that a little hamlet called Clovenfords, approximately six miles (ten kilometres) from Walkerburn came to my attention. Even though this is another very pretty little village, it is not exactly adjacent to the Tweed, and therefore it is not directly linked to the river or the story I am telling. However by chance, when I delved into the history of Clovenfords that's when I was taken by surprise, especially as what I discovered is so unusual, that I had to read it at least twice to make sure of the facts. It is now highly likely that there are all sorts of possibilities running through your mind as to what it was that took me completely unawares regarding what Clovenfords, could offer, I am therefore not going to keep you in suspense any longer, and tell you it was vineyards... yes you have read that correctly, vineyards.

Vineyards and Scotland are two words that generally do not sit well together, as given its northerly position and the often less than Mediterranean style weather which can be fairly normal for this area, it is not really the ideal conditions for growing grapes. However in the middle to late 19th Century this little hamlet was the toast of the U.K. and a large part of Europe as well, due to the quality of the grapes and ultimately the wine it produced.

The vineyards were established by the then head gardener for the Duke of Buccleuch, a very wealthy land owner with vast estates in the area. The grapes were grown under cover in what was basically a series of large greenhouses. The temperatures inside these greenhouses were controlled by miles of pipes which carried warm water round the roots of the plants The grapes were available for about six months of the year from late summer through until the early part of the following year and in a good year the harvest was reckoned to be in the region of fifteen thousand pounds in weight. Given that, as a rough guide it takes between two and three pounds of grapes to make a standard bottle of wine, this little village was capable of producing five thousand bottles of wine per year. This is possibly not a huge amount compared to the mass production facilities of say the French estates these days but in the 1880's this surely must have been quite an achievement. The six months of the year between grape harvests were not wasted either as the greenhouses were utilised to grow a large range of flowers and vegetables. The flowers, shrubs, cucumbers, lettuce and tomatoes which were grown, as well as various other products were shipped by rail on a daily basis to Edinburgh and London. Regretfully once again this wonderfully out of the ordinary business enterprise is no longer in existence although it did last for nearly one hundred years, before finally closing in 1959. Very close to Clovenfords but situated on the southern bank of the River Tweed is a grand country house known as Ashiestiel, there had been a building on this site from at least the middle of the 17th Century but its significance with regard to our story is that for a period of eight years from 1804 until 1812 it was inhabited by Walter Scott, of whom we shall learn considerably more in a few chapters time when we arrive at Abbotsford, the house he built and worked in up until his death in 1832. Walter Scott was, by the time he moved into Ashiestel Sheriff Depute of Selkirk and it was a requirement of the Judiciary system at that time that the Sheriff had to live in the vicinity of the courthouse where he presided and so it was that Scott moved from his current residence in Edinburgh, nearer to Selkirk. He rented Ashiestiel from his cousin Colonel Russell, Hugh Scott, Esq. who was serving in the British Army in India. It was whilst he lived in the house that Scott wrote "Marmion" an epic poem about a catastrophic defeat inflicted on the Scots by the English army in 1513 at Flodden. Once again we will read more about the battle itself and the resultant consequences for Scotland as we move further downstream and ever nearer to the actual battle site. Contained in the first Canto (a break in a long poem, similar to chapters in a book) of Marmion is a description in verse of a stream that ran through the grounds of Ashiestiel House. Walter Scott's ability to produce descriptive verse was widely recognized and he was often inspired by nature and the everyday things that surrounded him, the following lines being a perfect example of how he was able to take a subject as simple as a babbling stream and the vegetation which had grown over it during the summer virtually obscuring it from view, then turning it into a classic piece of poetry.

November's sky is chill and drear,
November's leaf is red and sear,
Late gazing down the steepy linn,
That hems our little garden in,
Low in it's dark and narrow glen,
You scarce the rivulet might ken,
So thick the tangled greenwood grew,
So feeble trill'd the streamlet through,
Now, murmuring hoarse, and frequent seen,
Through bush and briar no longer green
An angry brook, it sweeps the glade,
Brawls over rock and wild cascade,
And, foaming brown with doubled speed,
Hurries its water to the Tweed.

(An extract from "Marmion" written by Sir Walter Scott.)

Returning to the banks of the Tweed after leaving Ashiestiel we continue downstream. The Tweed has by now become a sizeable river, a "must visit" destination for fisherman from not only the UK but from all over the world. They can quite easily pay several hundred pounds per day to fish for salmon in the Tweed, such is the reputation of this river and its fishing. These sportsmen can sometimes be seen wading in the river up to their waists or perhaps even up to their chests in the water, ever wary of currents and eddies whilst all the time trying to tempt the inhabitants of these deep dark pools and gently flowing waters to grab the lures being offered to them. It is these pools which are the hiding and resting places of not only the native brown trout but also the migrating Atlantic salmon. The Latin name for the Atlantic salmon is "Salmo Salar" which translates to "the leaper" and describes perfectly this beautiful silver fish's actions as it makes its way upriver to its spawning ground. The lures used by the fishermen are usually imitation flies, made from a number of items but mainly fur, feathers, tinsel and thread. The ability to tie flies is an art in itself, to be able to transform a cold stark metal hook into an item that actually bears a resemblance to something natural is a wonder to marvel at. Even the names of these flies have a certain magical quality about them, how can you fail to marvel at the likes of Garry Dog, Jock Scott, Purple Shrimp and Thunder and Lightning which are designed for salmon fishing, whilst flies for trout fishing which are much smaller in size include names such as Blae and Black, March Brown, Partridge and Yellow, and Greenwells Glory.

The salmon is an extremely unusual and interesting fish, if only for the fact that it is able to adapt from being in fresh water at birth, to living in the salty ocean, for up to three or four years, and then returning to fresh water again, to reproduce. During the period they spend at sea, the salmon increases considerably in size, all the while building up their strength and fat reserves, to enable them to have the stamina to return once again to fresh water and in particular the river where they were born in order to spawn.

The Atlantic salmon's life begins as an egg, covered by fine gravel in a small stream which in this particular instance would be a tributary of the Tweed. The eggs are laid by the female salmon in a hollow called a Redd which she has dug out using her tail and body, utilising the strength of the current to move the gravel. The male salmon then fertilises the eggs and re-covers them with gravel to prevent them from being washed away. The eggs remain in the Redd over winter from November to March and when they hatch in Spring they are known as Alevins. There are then a number of different development stages in the young salmon's life which see it grow from an Alevin to Fry, then to Parr and finally a Smolt. In the Tweed, because of its nutrient rich water, a Smolt will be about twelve or thirteen centimetres long (approx. five/six inches) and have taken two to three years to reach this size. The rate of growth from Alevins to Smolt depends on a number of factors including water temperature and the availability of food. At this juncture they are also changing in appearance, up until now they have been very similar to trout, even having red spots on their flanks, but now they are turning silver and becoming much more like the adult fish. The Smolt stage is when the young salmon, are preparing to leave the river and head out to sea.

During their two to three years in the river they have gradually worked their way downstream and are now in the brackish waters of the estuary at Berwick-on-Tweed, waiting for a strong, high ebb tide to take them well away from the coast, where they will find the currents which will then take them relatively close to the Norwegian coast. They travel North up the coast of Norway to the Faroe Islands feeding all the time on sand eels, crustaceans, herring and other fish species. They may very well spend up to a year in this location and it has been known for some of these fish to then return to the river of their birth. At this stage they are known as grilse, however returning after one year is fairly unusual and more often than not what is likely to happen is that the majority of salmon move further westwards towards Greenland and continue feeding in the food rich waters off the south and west coasts of that island. Salmon are voracious feeders during their time at sea and as a result increase in size dramatically. After approximately three years at sea, the urge to return to their birth river takes a hold and they begin the long journey back. Records of salmon caught which have been tagged, show that they tend to come back via the western coast of Ireland but at this point data becomes very sparse. We can only assume that they then travel round the northern shores of Ireland and Scotland and use the currents which are predominant in the centre of the North Sea to carry them southwards. Once again, information from tagged fish that have been caught show that some Tweed salmon at least, travel as far south as Northumberland, in the North of England then turn in towards the coast and head back Northwards to the river in which they were born. When they reach the mouth of the river of their choice, it then depends on the amount of water in the river, whether or not they can proceed any further. If necessary they will wait in the estuary until there is sufficient water flow or the river is in flood to enable them to travel up-river and the whole process starts again. The number of eggs produced by each female fish varies depending on her size, the bigger the fish the more eggs she will produce, but generally it is an average of five thousand eggs. This at first seems to be an enormous amount of eggs, but the attrition rate for eggs and indeed the young fish in their early stages of life is extremely high, mainly through natural predators. The dangers, do not decrease for the salmon, as they get bigger however, because now in addition to their natural enemies, they are hunted by humans as well, indulging in both commercial and sporting fishing.

Continuing our downstream travels, the river passes through the Yair estate and flows past the very impressive looking Yair House. The name Yair comes from an old Scottish word meaning fish trap. Permission was given in 1156 by King Malcolm of Scotland, to the monks from Kelso abbey to build a dam and create a fishing pool in the River Tweed. Why they decided to build it at Yair is not known as this is some considerable distance from Kelso Abbey even by today's standards and one would certainly think that there were a number of equally good sites on the Tweed for a fish trap much nearer the Abbey itself. It was here however that the pool was built and this in turn then gave the "Yair" estate its name. The Georgian style Yair house was built in1788 by Alexander Pringle who had made his fortune in India and used his money to buy the Yair estates which had needed to be sold earlier that century to pay off massive debts. The house sits back from the river but has marvellous views both upstream and down. The Yair bridge is a three span "A" listed stone bridge built in 1764 which crosses the Tweed just below Yair House and carries the main A707 road from Peebles to Selkirk, it is at this point that we will leave the course of the Tweed and deviate from the route a little to visit Selkirk and Hawick, two of the Borders biggest towns.

Whilst the theme of the book and the stories within it relate principally to the River Tweed and what happens on its banks, I did mention right at the beginning when we were in Moffat that occasionally we would have to travel a little bit further afield if that was required and this is one of these occasions. Neither Selkirk nor Hawick could be described as being next to the Tweed, however the rivers that flow through these Border towns are in fact tributaries of the Tweed so there is a loose connection. The real reason for visiting these towns is that a journey through the Borders without visiting either of them would indeed be an opportunity missed.

THE GRADE 2 LISTED YAIR BRIDGE

CHAPTER 5

selkirk & hawick

Selkirk sits on rolling hills over looking the Ettrick River, which joins the Tweed three miles (five kilometres) further East and once again it was the river that provided the power for industry in Selkirk, first of all in the production of leather goods, in particular shoes, then tweed and textile manufacturing which started in the middle to late 18th century. Whilst most of this industry, has to all intents and purposes ceased as a major employer of people in the area, a certain amount of production still continues.

Even before proper asphalt paved roads became the norm Selkirk was situated on one of the main routes between England and Scotland and was therefore often at the receiving end of death and destruction by both English and Scottish raiding parties. Like so many of the other villages and towns in Scotland a considerable number of Selkirk's young men were slaughtered by the English at the Battle of Flodden in 1513. With nobody to defend the town it was ransacked by at least some of the soldiers from the victorious English army. Philiphaugh, a relatively flat piece of land a short distance from the town of Selkirk itself, was the scene of another fierce battle in September 1645 when Sir David Leslie commander of the Covenanter forces made a surprise early morning attack on the Marquis of Montrose's Royalist force. The Covenanters were a group of people determined

to keep the Presbyterian religion alive in Scotland. They had signed a Covenant to confirm their opposition to interference by the Stuart kings whose belief it was that they were the spiritual heads of the Church of Scotland, whereas the Covenanters believed that only Jesus Christ could be the head of a Christian Church.

The Royalist army under the command of Montrose had been enjoying a successful campaign in Scotland with several victories under their belt, the latest being at Kilsyth. This in effect had destroyed the Covenanters resistance in Scotland. The lowland towns were now at his mercy but various disputes among his commanders had resulted in many of his troops leaving and returning to their homes. Montrose then made the decision to lead his depleted force into the Borders, hoping to recruit more men and bring his army back up to strength. When Montrose reached Selkirk he had his men set up camp on this fairly flat piece of ground near Selkirk known as Philiphaugh. Such was the confidence of the Royalists from their recent victories, that most of the Royalist army officers and commanders had decided to find more comfortable accommodation in the town of Selkirk itself which was nearly a mile away from where the soldiers were camped. When the attack by Leslie started on a rather foggy autumn morning, it took the Royalist forces completely by surprise and because their officers were not there, confusion was rife. Even when their commanders became aware of the situation and did eventually get to the battlefield, heavy losses had been suffered and as a result it was not so much a battle, more a massacre. Even the troops who surrendered after being promised clemency were killed in cold blood along with all their camp followers. These days Philiphaugh is still an area where fierce battles take place on a regular basis but the battles these days tend to be more in the form of a sporting nature as the area is now home to Selkirk's rugby and cricket teams and the local derbies especially, provide hotly contested and entertaining matches.

A SEA TROUT FOLLOWED BY A SALMON NEGOTIATING A FISH LADDER

SITE OF SIR WALTER SCOTT'S COURT HOUSE, SELKIRK

In 2005 a salmon viewing centre was opened at the site and using various cameras located around the area, it is possible to watch the salmon negotiate the cauld (Scottish word for weir) adjacent to the Yarrow and Ettrick Rivers as they battle their way upstream against the current to reach their spawning grounds. The centre is open all year round but the best time for salmon viewing is in the Autumn from September to November. Salmon are not the only wildlife that can be viewed on a visit to Philiphaugh, there are various walks available around the area of differing lengths, so, depending on your fitness level and the time at your disposal it is possible to see red squirrel, roe deer, heron and a multitude of other bird life depending on the season.

Sir Walter Scott, about whom we shall hear more soon, when we travel past his house at Abbotsford was Sheriff of Selkirk from 1799 until 1832. This position was perhaps the equivalent of today's magistrate and a very important post. The courthouse where Sir Walter presided, is today a tourist attraction and open to the public. Another famous son of Selkirk is Mungo Park, who attended Edinburgh University studying medicine and botany. In 1793 he took an oral examination with The Royal College of Surgeons of England which he passed with flying colours. In 1794 he offered his services to the African Association and in 1795 was selected to lead an expedition to discover the course of the Niger river. Unfortunately it was an unsuccessful mission for various reasons, but failed mainly due to disease and lack of resources. He returned to Scotland and used his medical knowledge to become a physician in Peebles. However that was nothing short of pure monotony for Mungo Park and in 1805 after being asked by the government to lead another African expedition set off from Portsmouth to Gambia. Once again, this new expedition's aim was an attempt to try and trace the route of the Niger River. The expedition encountered many difficulties, especially disease which killed a large number of the party. Sailing down the Niger, Mungo's party was confronted at various times by groups of hostile natives and it was during one of these attacks that he was forced along with three others to abandon their canoe and try to swim to safety. Unfortunately this was a particularly rough part of the river with a fierce current and Mungo along with the others in his party were drowned apart from one native who survived and was able to tell his rescuers what had happened. Mungo Parks' remains are buried on the banks of the Niger near Jabba, Nigeria.

Close to Selkirk is Bowhill House and Park, home to The Duke and Duchess of Buccleuch and Queensberry. The present Bowhill House has existed since 1812 but family connections in the area extend over seven centuries. The house and grounds are open to the public and amongst the attractions at Bowhill, is an open air theatre. Seating less than a hundred people, the audience have a feeling of intimacy with the cast, whilst enjoying an ever changing variety of professional shows. Inside Bowhill House itself, there is a priceless collection of French antiques and European paintings, including works by Gainsborough, Reynolds and Canaletto.

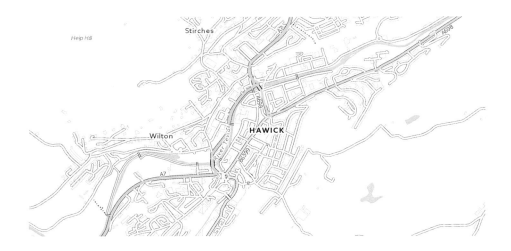

Having only told you about a small part of Selkirk's history but hopefully having whetted your appetite to discover more we now leave the town and travel west along the A7 towards our next stop. It would be difficult to travel through the Borders and miss out on the opportunity to visit Hawick, arguably the Borders most famous and biggest town. Hawick is less than ten miles (sixteen kilometres) from Selkirk and in geographical terms sits more or less directly in the middle of the Scottish Borders, being roughly forty five miles(seventy two kilometres) from Carlisle in the West and fifty five miles (eighty eight kilometres) from Edinburgh, Scotland's capital on the East coast.

Hawick is a Borders town with a long and chequered history. There was an Angles settlement here in Hawick as far back as the 600's, and after The Battle of Hastings in 1066 the victorious Norman Lords started to acquire land and estates throughout England and Scotland. It was in this period that the Lovells family built a fortified tower in the area. Because of its central position Hawick was constantly involved in the cross border feuds which were prevalent between 1300 and 1600. It has been mentioned in previous pages that Border towns suffered more than most with regard to losses incurred at The Battle of Flodden in 1513, and Hawick is no exception, but it cannot be over emphasized just how much devastation was caused by the loss of so many men of fighting age. In a short while as we move further downstream we will be considerably closer to the site of the Battle of Flodden and I will reveal more details of the events that occurred on this dramatic day in Scottish History, a day in which Scotland lost its King, most of its nobility, and thousands of its ordinary population. A year after the Battle of Flodden in 1514, a raiding party of English troops were surprised by a group of very young Hawick men who not only engaged them in

combat but beat them and captured their standard. This event is celebrated every year when several hundred riders take part in "The Hawick Common Riding." This is a traditional ride around the boundaries of the burgh to make sure that the adjoining towns and landowners have not encroached on land belonging to Hawick and that there is no threat to the town from its enemies. Whilst the likelihood of boundaries being changed and the residents of Hawick being threatened have long since gone, it is an annual event celebrated usually in early June and attracts not only the local population, but residents from the other Border towns, as well as tourists and ex-pats on holiday.

Hawicks' fame, prosperity and fortune over the last few hundred years has been built round its textile industry. In the middle to late 1600 's it was mainly socks which were produced, all hand knitted but still very much a cottage industry. By the 1770's hand knitting machines were being replaced by powered machinery driven by water from the Slitrig and Teviot rivers which flow through Hawick. The flow of the rivers were diverted via a complex arrangement of lades and sluices through the textile mills, providing not only power for the machinery but a constant supply of water to wash the fleeces. The first knitting frames were installed in Hawick in 1771 by Bailie John Hardie and by the 1840's over a thousand were being used, producing over a million pairs of stockings a year. By the middle of the 19th century when water power was being replaced by steam power there were several thousand workers producing not just hosiery but also carpets, underwear, and all sorts of woollen and linen goods and this was when names widely associated with luxury textile products started to appear, names such as Pringle, Lyle and Scott, Peter Scott and John Laing, along with many other household names some of whom are still evident today.

By 1849 Hawick had a rail connection with Edinburgh and that, plus a better system of roads, meant that bringing raw materials in and taking the finished products away was considerably easier. In 1862 a further rail connection was made to Carlisle, which already had a main line connection to London. This provided the Hawick textile industry with even bigger marketing opportunities. Textiles however, whilst being by far the main employer in the town, was not the only business that Hawick had as this vibrant Borders town was also the central hub for a livestock market and by the 1920's nearly three hundred thousand sheep and cattle were being sold annually at this market, before being shipped to various destinations by road and rail. Unfortunately the infamous Doctor Beeching and his railway closures in the late sixties, resulted in Hawick losing its rail link, and this in turn meant the gradual decline of the livestock market. The area of ground where animals were bought and sold is now a supermarket, perhaps therefore it is as busy as it previously was, but the smell, the noise, the atmosphere and the excitement which was the livestock market has gone. There have always, been groups actively campaigning for the return of a railway service to the Borders and it does now appear that all their hard work has not been in vain. There is at present what appears to be a very good chance that a railway connection could once again be established between Edinburgh and Galashiels another of the large Border towns which we will be visiting soon. This link is possibly going to be in place and working as early as 2015. Sadly it will not extend as far as Hawick, although I am sure that the various groups involved will continue to pressure local councils and governments to try and achieve this.

Hawick has given birth to a number of famous people and quite surprisingly motor cycling champions feature very strongly, the first being Andrew James Guthrie (1897-1937) better known perhaps as "Jimmie Guthrie" winner of nineteen Grand Prix's, six Isle of Man TT wins and three wins in the North West 200. Jimmie's exploits on the track, were followed by Steve Hislop (1962 – 2003) who claimed no less than eleven Isle of Man TT wins and in 1989 became the first rider to average over 120mph around the thirty seven and three quarter mile mountain circuit. He had an epic battle in 1991 at the Isle of Man with another motorcycle racing God called Carl Fogarty who later went on to win several World G.P. titles but on this occasion he could not match the aggressive riding which was Hislop's trademark style. He was also British Superbike Champion twice and won races in World Superbikes and World Endurance Racing but regretfully was killed in a helicopter crash in the Borders in 2003.One of Steve Hislop's protégés another Hawick born racer called Stuart Easton has already had a considerable amount of success, winning the Supersport title back in 2002 and numerous other wins since. An extremely serious crash which left him with multiple injuries restricted his racing for some considerable time, but the good news is he has made a complete recovery and will hopefully soon be back on the top of the podium.

Its not just motorcyclists from Hawick who have gained fame, included in the list of other greats are people such as Bill McLaren "the voice of rugby", Dame Isobel Baillie, Soprano, Sir Chay Blyth, single handed sailor, Nigel Griffiths, former labour politician, Sir James Murray, Lexicographer, and Anne Redpath, Artist. Anne was actually born in Galashiels but spent a considerable amount of her time in Hawick and so has been adopted by the town as one of their own.

CHAPTER 6

abbotsford, sir walter scott

Back on our travels once again and less than fifteen miles from Hawick by road is Abbotsford, the magnificent home of Sir Walter Scott, renowned the world over for his historical poems and books. Abbotsford House sits atop terraced grass banks which overlook fields leading down to the River Tweed providing views that estate agents today would probably classify as "to die for" Walter Scott was born in 1771 and grew up in Scotland's capital city, Edinburgh. He developed polio at a young age which left him with a pronounced limp and it was through extended visits to his grandfathers farm in the Borders for curative sessions that an interest developed not only in his family history but also the Borders and its culture. During one of these extended visits he attended the local grammar school in Kelso, there he met James and John Ballantyne, two brothers who were later to become not only his publishers but also his business partners. He continued his education in Edinburgh and took a law degree at Edinburgh University, following in his father's footsteps. It was in Edinburgh, that he was called to the bar in 1792. During the years he spent studying for his law degree he met another of Scotland's famous poet sons, Robert Burns. They met at a literary workshop organized by one of Scott's professors from Edinburgh University. As far as records show, this was their one and only recorded encounter. The next five years for Scott were spent

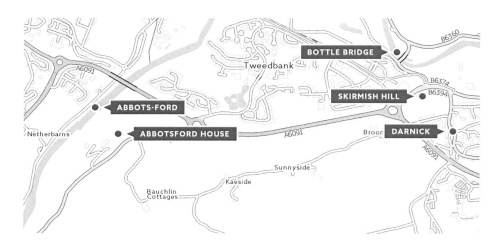

translating poetry works from German into English and he also started writing his own poetry. He married Charlotte Charpentier (Carpenter) in 1797, his wife was the daughter of a French refugee and together they had five children.

In 1802 Sir Walter showed how his future writings were going to develop by publishing a collection of historical Scottish ballads called "The Minstrelsy of the Scottish Borders", contained in a three volume set. Scott was, if nothing else, extremely hard working and continued with his law career as well as his writing. He also became Sheriff of Selkirk and Principal Clerk at the Court of Session in Edinburgh, he published reviews, started a theatre in Edinburgh, and still managed to find time to edit various works, as well as making anonymous contributions to the Tory Quarterly Review.

Scott's writings had up to this point been mainly poetry, and his early publications were being printed by his aforementioned friends James and John Ballantyne. The printing was at that time being done at the Ballantyne brothers workshop in Kelso, although Scott was later going to persuade them to move to Edinburgh. It was in 1805 when "The Lay of the Last Minstrel" was printed that Scott's works caught the attention of the public and it was then that Scott's reputation as a poet and writer gained him celebrity status. There are many well known proverbs in colloquial English and when "Marmion" was published in 1808 two lines from this poem found their way into everyday life and speech

"Oh what a tangled web we weave ,

when first we practice to deceive"

In 1810 "The Lady of the Lake" was published and translated into German, extracts were then selected and set to music by Franz Schubert, Scott's popularity was growing at a pace.

Poetry was considered, at the time, by his father and the public in general to be the only way of relating stories especially of an historic nature. Novels were regarded as rather common, so not wanting to upset his father, Scott's first novel was published anonymously. It is a story of Jacobites and Whigs, (an anti Catholic political party) love and romance, bravery, battles, chivalry and treason all the elements which inspired so many of his novels and these were woven round historical facts and real events. The result was "Waverley", published in 1814.

This was followed over the next five years by a number of other books with a similar theme involving a historical Scottish background. It has been suggested that Scott had always wanted to be a soldier, but his childhood illness had put paid to that. His books and poems with tales of chivalry, fighting and battles were his way of realizing his childhood ambitions. Always mindful of the reputation he had gained as a poet the rest of these books which collectively became known as "The Waverley Novels" were also published anonymously. However his style of writing was known to quite a few of his friends and family and the identity of the author of the Waverley Novels became an open secret and in 1815 he was invited to have dinner with George, The Prince Regent, who was anxious to meet the author

VIEW OF ABBOTSFORD HOUSE, WITH THE EILDON HILLS IN BACKGROUND

of these books. With such distinguished people seeking his friendship, Scott was not only propelled to literary fame in Scotland and the United Kingdom but also Europe and America and it was these tales of chivalry, romance and gallantry which rank him, many people say alongside Shakespeare as one of the literary greats of the period.

If you are reading this and wondering why I seem to be spending more time, devoting more space and going into more detail about Abbotsford and Sir Walter than any other part of the book so far, then I suppose at this point I should confess my interest and fascination for Abbotsford and Sir Walter Scott. I said in the opening chapters that my formative years were spent in the Borders and in fact this was at Abbotsford. My parents and my elder sister and I moved there when I was three years old, we stayed in a cottage on the estate and I lived there for sixteen years before moving to Edinburgh. My father was employed by the Abbotsford Estate and his "bosses" were Mrs Patricia Maxwell Scott and her younger sister by two years Dame Jean Maxwell Scott, both great great great granddaughters of Sir Walter Scott himself. In 1954 their father, Major-General Sir Walter-Constable-Maxwell Scott died and the two sisters inherited the Abbotsford Estate.

It was obvious when they inherited Abbotsford, that a house and grounds of that size needed large sums of money to maintain and repair it. Their main source of income was from the thousands of tourists who came to Abbotsford, from all over the world, to look at Sir Walter Scott's collections. As well as being an author and poet, he was an avid collector, not just of books and poetry, but weapons, armour, clothes, and paintings as well as hundreds of items he had been given by friends or collected during his travels around the globe. Sir Walter's personal library at Abbotsford on its own contains more than nine thousand books.

The figures for visitor numbers increased significantly after both Miss Jean and Mrs Patricia Maxwell Scott did a promotional tour of America and by the late 70's and early 80's Abbotsford was attracting eighty thousand visitors a year. This was a huge number of visitors, given that the museum was only open for a limited period, usually April to September each year.

There was a significant moment in 1962 when electricity was installed at Abbotsford, as up until then the only source of power for cooking and lighting had been from a mains gas supply. The big switch on was a huge occasion with press, television and many dignitaries in attendance. Abbotsford House was illuminated by a series of floodlights and the house looked spectacular. We of course, by that I mean my parents, my sister and I had our own little celebration in our cottage. I was nearly twelve years old by then and we were able to watch television in our own house for the first time. What a thrill, it was even if the picture was only in black and white and an extremely small screen by today's standards, but it was a television.

Life at Abbotsford as a youngster was, having the ability to look back, idyllic. Whilst at first the significance of Sir Walter Scott did not register with me, it was perhaps the fascination of several hundred people per day during the summer months visiting "where I lived" that made

RIVER TWEED, ABBOTSFORD

it special. The tiny car park, a hundred yards or so from where our cottage stood was often jam packed with tour buses based in Edinburgh, which brought hordes of mainly Americans and Japanese but also lots of other nationalities as well, to visit the museum and gardens. By the time I was six or seven years old I had picked up enough of the salient points regarding Abbotsford, Sir Walter and the countryside round about to be able to give a passable talk to these unfortunate tourists who knocked on our cottage door when the museum was closed, hoping we could somehow produce the necessary keys to open everything up for them.

Sometimes, if we (my father or myself) were not busy, they would strike it lucky, because we could tell them about, and show them places that were normally out of bounds to the everyday visitors. There was the secret underground passage which went from one side of Abbotsford to the other, but unfortunately a roof fall had blocked it just over halfway through, but it was still exciting to venture even half way through, especially when you were only a seven year old. There was the walled garden with walls nearly two feet thick in places. These walls though were hollow inside and at various points in the wall, bricks could be removed so that fires could be lit inside. The gardeners in the days of Sir Walter, would light these fires in the winter or when it was frosty. The hot air from the fires would then circulate around inside the walls and keep the frost from damaging the early blossoms on the various fruit trees which lined the walls inside the garden. My first thoughts at that tender age, when I learnt about the fires, was that it seemed to be a lot of trouble to go to just to be able to have a few apples, plums or pears, but of course in the days of Sir Walter, perishable items such as fruit and vegetables were not so readily available all year round as they are today. There would certainly have been a glut when the harvest was ready but in order

ABBOTSFORD HOUSE AND GARDENS

to have a supply for the months ahead the crop or at least some of it would have to be preserved in storage jars. Then there were the cellars, deep underground which in Sir Walter's time used to be filled with great mounds of snow and ice in the winter, meat, could then be hung in the cellars and the snow and ice would keep it cool and reasonably fresh until well into the following year, was this then the first refrigeration concept? Then finally gas, Sir Walter Scott was very much tuned in to modern ideas and he had installed gas lighting and a revolutionary under floor heating system at Abbotsford which made it one of the first houses in Scotland if not the whole U.K. to utilize gas in this way. Hidden away at the rear of Abbotsford House when I lived there was one of the original gas containers, a huge heavy iron container over four feet high, supposedly lead lined which was the gas container of that period, so far removed from today's containers which can be easily transported as to make it virtually unrecognizable. Our family cottage was situated in the grounds of Abbotsford and adjacent to the route used by the many visitors as they walked from the car park to the museum. The wooden gate which led into our garden had a wonderful thick rail running along the bottom which meant that if I stood on it, I was able to see over the top of the gate. Quite often I would be standing on the gate at the entrance to our garden, just watching the different nationalities pass by and occasionally chatting to them in the way that only five year olds can. At that age I was also quite photogenic, with a mass of curly hair framing my face, so having my photograph taken was a fairly regular occurrence, unfortunately neither of these childhood traits, the curly hair or the photogenic face have followed me into adult life. It is at this point that I have to make a confession and apologize to an unknown number of tourists who on one particular day handed over to me considerable amounts of cash in exchange for a ticket which I gave them, allowing them admission to Sir Walter Scott's museum. The problem was that these tickets I was handing out, had been carelessly dropped by previous visitors and I had collected them, (well that's what little boys do isn't it?) I was merely holding them in my hand. The tickets had the entry price to the museum stamped on them and as I handed them to the visitors they gave me money, which at the time, seemed to me anyway, to be a very fair exchange indeed. It was only when they reached the entrance to the museum and showed their "entry" ticket to the cashier that my money making enterprise was rumbled. Needless to say, when my mother was informed by concerned staff from the museum, my business ceased trading very rapidly. My extremely embarrassed mother tried to re-unite the cash with its rightful owners, but I seem to re-call seeing a number of the visitors just shaking their heads, whilst laughing , pointing and smiling at me. Smiling incidentally, was something that I personally did not manage for quite a few days after that incident. I will leave it to your imagination as to the reasons why I wasn't able to sit down very comfortably either.

Having been away from Abbotsford and the Borders for many, many years with only infrequent visits to remind me of what I was missing, I can reflect back on those carefree days as a youngster, climbing trees, playing at cowboys or outlaws, maybe even on a good day imagining being one of the great Scottish heroes, Rob Roy McGregor, William Wallace, or Robert the Bruce, riding bikes through the woods before mountain biking was even thought of, fishing in the River Tweed from dawn to dusk for those elusive brown trout (it would cost a fortune to do that today). Tobogganing down seemingly vertical slopes in the winter when the snow was often knee high and it was impossible to go to school. Those were the days before health and safety became a watch word and children were allowed to play properly, it was great fun...I still have the scars today to prove it!!

Anyway I digress, back to the subject. Sir Walter Scott continued to provide an ample supply of books and poems and his fame grew accordingly and it was because of his popularity that the Prince Regent, the future King George IV gave permission to Scott to try and find the long lost Crown Jewels of Scotland which had been secreted away during the Cromwell years and subsequently lost. So it was in 1818 that Scott and a small team of soldiers who had been searching the inner depths of Edinburgh Castle, found the Crown Jewels, much to the delight of the Prince Regent. In fact, he was so grateful that he granted Scott the title of Baronet, and it was when George was King that Sir Walter Scott was asked to provide the pageantry for the Kings visit to Scotland in 1822, the first visit by a reigning British Monarch for over 170 years. This he managed to do very successfully despite having been given only a very short time, less than three weeks in fact, to arrange everything. He even managed to dress the visiting Royal party, including the King in tartan. This was indeed a significant event considering King George's previous relationships with the Scots, particularly the Highlanders who after the 1745 Jacobite rebellion had been forbidden to wear clan tartans or carry swords. This law had only been relaxed in 1782 but the wearing of tartan was very much still regarded, especially by the English, as only being clothing fit for the lower classes. The King's visit, however and the fact that he wore a tartan outfit which in todays' money would have cost well over £100,000 pounds had elevated the material to be a fashion must have, worn by anybody who could muster even the faintest connection to a clan. It was in this period that Scott commissioned a pair of trousers to be made for himself in "shepherds check" a fairly small black and white check in a tweed material. This soon became very popular and other colours of this pattern evolved such as heather and granite variants. The clothes produced from this material, because of their hard wearing characteristics were now worn by wealthier members of society for their hunting, shooting, fishing and deerstalking activities and soon spread not just throughout Scotland and England but all over the world. The feel good factor of the Kings visit to Scotland and the reception he received not only from the Lowland Scots but also from the Highlander Clan chiefs was a pleasant surprise to the King and was in no small way down to the management of the occasion by Sir Walter.

Unfortunately in 1825 matters took a turn for the worst for Sir Walter when a financial crisis involving the banks in London and Edinburgh caused major problems (nothing seems to have changed then) and in particular with the printing business of the Ballantyne brothers who had moved to Edinburgh and with whom Scott was now in partnership. Although he had many offers of financial help from his friends and admirers, Scott refused them all as it would have meant declaring himself bankrupt and that could have threatened his ownership of one of his most treasured possessions Abbotsford House. He decided instead that the way to clear his debts would be to write more books, poems and articles for papers and magazines.

He also decided to place his beloved Abbotsford and his literary income in a trust which would belong to his creditors. Determined to pay off his debts and despite failing health he undertook a tour of Europe which proved to be hugely popular and he was welcomed and praised wherever he went. On his return to Scotland and Abbotsford, however his health deteriorated even further and he died in September 1832 aged sixty one. Sir Walter still owed a substantial sum of money to his creditors but as his books and poems continued to sell the outstanding debts on his estate were eventually discharged.

Sir Walter Scott's body was laid to rest at Dryburgh Abbey, close to one of his favourite places to stop on his travels through the Borders, an area which was later to become known as Scott's View. It is a spot high on a hill overlooking a great horseshoe shaped bend on the River Tweed with the Eildon Hills on the far horizon and mile upon mile of beautiful Border countryside in between. After the deaths of Mrs Patricia Maxwell Scott (1998) and Dame Jean Maxwell Scott (2004) there was no one else to inherit the estate as they were the last of the line of direct descendants.

Abbotsford House and its grounds are now in the care of a Trust which was started in 2007. They have raised a considerable amount of money through grants and donations and are embarking on a huge renovation project which includes not only work on Abbotsford House itself, but also the gardens and grounds. A new Visitor centre is being built which will include a restaurant and gift shop. Plans are also in place to provide luxury accommodation available for those who want to have a short break at the house in which Sir Walter Scott lived and worked. It is hoped that all this work will be completed and ready for the new tourist season of 2013. Abbotsford as a name is known and used in many countries worldwide including America, Canada, Australia, New Zealand and South Africa and there are at least three streets in London with Abbotsford in the title, a fitting tribute indeed to the man whose stories and poems made the name famous.

Half a mile or so downstream from Abbotsford house is Abbots Ford itself, a relatively shallow stretch of the river Tweed, the river at this point is also fairly slow flowing, which made it much easier for horse drawn wagons and carts to cross, as well as people on foot. The name Abbot's Ford is thought to come from the fact that Abbots from Melrose Abbey used to cross the river here. Upgrading of the Borders road system in relatively recent times, has seen the construction of a bridge to carry the main road from Galashiels to Melrose over the River Tweed, just a few yards downstream from the Abbots Ford itself.

RIVER TWEED, ABBOTSFORD

CHAPTER 7

galashiels, bottle bridge, skirmish hill

The town of Galashiels is situated on the opposite side of the river Tweed to Abbotsford. It derives its name from "Shielings by the Gala" meaning dwelling or place to stay and was often accompanied by another name in this case Gala so the two together meant houses beside the Gala water. The River Gala yet another major tributary of the River Tweed merges with the river just a short distance below Abbots Ford itself.

First mentioned in 1124 during the reign of David 1 of Scotland, Galashiels is another Border town which relied heavily on the textile industry to provide employment for its population. From the early 1700's the manufacture of woollen cloth had taken place here with power for the machinery provided by the river Gala which bi-sects the town. The woollen goods produced at that time were mainly a fairly coarse type of cloth manufactured from the fleeces of local sheep. By the mid 1800's however, Galashiels had a railway line with a direct link to Edinburgh. This meant that the woollen mills were able to obtain fleeces not only from other parts of Britain but also imported wool as well. Using a mixture of these other fleeces with the local wool produced a much finer quality cloth which was also extremely hard wearing and was arguably a better quality of material than that which was being manufactured in various parts of England and Wales. The railways were also bringing

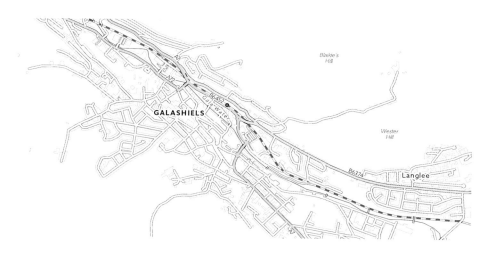

into the area supplies of fuel, namely coal. Coal, as well as providing heating for homes was another source of power for the woollen mills and the railway proved to be the ideal transport medium not only for bringing raw materials and fuel in to Galashiels, but also to take the finished product away to the wider markets in Edinburgh and from there to London and the rest of the world. An interesting comment was discovered whilst looking for information regarding the wool and hosiery industries. It had been noted that very occasionally unusual plants, grasses, wild flowers and even weeds could be spotted along the banks of the River Gala, varieties which were not native to Scotland or even the United Kingdom. After much deliberation the theory was put forward that seeds imbedded in the imported fleeces had been released into the river during the washing process, these had eventually come to rest in the soil at the river's edge and taken root. These exotic plant variants never became really established however due in the main part to Scotland's inhospitable climate compared to where they had originated from.

A guide as to how much of an impact the arrival of the railway had in the Borders and in particular Galashiels is reflected in the following figures, which shows not only the dramatic increase in mill production units but also the population. In 1788 there were ten textile manufacturers, and by 1825 this had increased to thirty five with a population of 1600. By 1891 the population was 18000 a figure which is even higher than today's count. Galashiels was also developing a reputation for quality products and during " The Great Exhibition of Industrial Products of Nations" in 1851 the manufacturers of Galashiels won no less than four medals for the excellence of their woollen products. The golden age of textile production has however passed and as with many other industries, there was fierce competition from abroad with cheaper products and cheaper labour costs. Whilst there is still a certain amount of high quality goods manufactured in a small number of outlets it is nothing like the amount previously produced. Galashiels though was better placed geographically than many of its local rivals and as a result has been able to develop other industries which have managed to counter job losses from the woollen mills. This unfortunately is something which in other towns we have visited, they have not been able to do as successfully as Galashiels. There is considerable local rivalry between the Border towns none more so than Galashiels and Hawick. Everything from their industries to their rugby and football teams compete strongly for top position.

At the time of writing Galashiels is the biggest of the Borders towns population wise and with the prospect of a rail link being re-established with Edinburgh by 2015 it is expected that Galashiels will expand even more. Galashiels is also home to the School of Textiles and Design, formerly The Scottish College of Textiles which became part of Heriot Watt University in the late 1990's and for many years has been teaching students from all over the world the intricacies of the textile industry, such as weaving, knitting, printing, fashion design, and computerized production. The number of courses available is also increasing year by year as demand for more and more subjects connected with the knitwear industry are asked for and so there are now also graduate courses in interior design and fashion communication.

Like the majority of the other Border Towns, Galashiels has its "Common Riding" which takes place normally towards the end of June beginning of July each year and consists of several hundred mounted men and women patrolling the boundaries of the Burgh stopping at various points of historical significance along the way. The group is led by "The Braw Lad" and his "Lass" who carry the Burgh flag which depicts two foxes at the base of a plum tree, this is supposedly a reference to when an English raiding party were caught unawares at a point close to Galashiels, as they rested under a wild plum tree enjoying the fruits. Needless to say this moment of relaxation did not last for very long and they were dealt with in no uncertain terms. The two principals are elected in the spring of each year to carry out the various duties required during the ceremonies in and around Galashiels and also to act as the town's ambassadors at the other Border towns' festivals.

Galashiels has been the birthplace of several famous people, not unexpectedly this includes quite a few rugby players, as the Borders favourite sporting pastime is indeed rugby and we will learn more about this very soon when we visit Melrose, another well known Border town. In the 1920's Andrew Murdison achieved fame by not only playing rugby union, which was then still played as an amateur sport, but also later becoming a paid professional rugby league player for Halifax. Craig Chalmers, Chris Patterson, Bryan Redpath, and Gregor Townsend are names which are probably more recognizable from the present day. John Collins and Danny Galbraith are both professional footballers. It is not just rugby and football players, born in Galashiels, however who have achieved fame, some other famous "Braw Lads and Lassies" are Russell Fairgrieve C.B.E. Conservative Politician, Captain Douglas Ford captured in Hong Kong by the Japanese in 1941 and awarded the George Cross for conspicuous gallantry. Judith Miller, Antiques Expert, who has written many books on the subject, Archibald Cochran Physician and Ryan Mania, Jockey and Grand National Winner in 2013.

We continue our downstream journey from Galashiels, and the next point of interest is just over a mile away. Lowood Bridge or the Bottle Bridge, as it is known locally was built in 1826 and it is suggested that the name comes from the fact that a bottle containing newspapers and coins dated from when the bridge was built is included somewhere in the brickwork. Another possible reason for the name is that both entrances to the bridge are relatively wide but then the bridge narrows in the middle giving it a bottle neck type shape. Because of the narrowness of the bridge, traffic flow is now controlled by traffic lights. A simple solution to reduce the number of "bumps" which used to occur on the bridge on a regular basis.

Five minutes walk from the Bottle Bridge will bring you to Skirmish Hill. It is now the site of a large hotel, but in July 1526 it was the scene of a bloody battle. Archibald Douglas, the Earl of Angus had put himself in the position of mentor for the then very young King James V. Neither King James himself or his closest supporters liked the influence that Douglas was able to exert over the young King, but there was apparently very little that could be done to alter the situation. However Walter Scott of Buccleugh (no relation to Sir Walter Scott) had decided that some action was necessary as it was feared that Archibald Douglas's control could alter the status quo. So it was therefore, that he with several hundred mounted supporters rode to a hamlet near Skirmish Hill called Darnick in an attempt to intercept Douglas and if necessary engage in a battle to free the King. The forces of both sides did meet and a skirmish developed (hence the name of the hill where the fighting took place). As the fighting started the young King James was spirited away from the danger to Darnick Tower a small fortified house in the hamlet of Darnick itself and it is said that he in fact watched the battle from the battlements of the tower. However Scott's challenge failed, one of the main reasons being that his troops were more used to cattle raids across the Border rather than organized toe to toe combat with a much more professional and better equipped foe. The end result was that the king remained under the influence of Douglas for several more years. With hundreds of dead on both sides this was a fairly significant but not very well documented battle and it is only recently that an information board, giving an account of the battle has been erected in the field near to where these two opposing forces met.

BRAW LAD AND LASS CROSSING RIVER TWEED AT ABBOTSFORD

THE BOTTLE BRIDGE

melrose, trimontium, hadrians wall melrose abbey, rugby

Once more we return to the banks of the River Tweed, and continue our journey downstream and soon arrive at Melrose which is less than two miles away. Melrose today is probably best known for its ruined Cistercian Abbey, Rugby Sevens Tournament, Pipe Band Contest and it's Book Festival. All these activities attract visitors in their thousands, but Melrose is also steeped in history and this can be traced as far back as 1500 B.C. when the nearby three peaks of the Eildon Hills, which dominate the town, were populated by Bronze Age Celts. There does seem to be a gap in recorded history after 900B.C. but there is also some evidence of Iron Age Settlers in and around the Melrose region. The relative peace of these times, if such a thing existed, was somewhat shattered by the arrival of the Romans in approximately 80AD. The Romans, well known for their construction expertise had built solid roads from Dover on the South Coast of England and as they had progressed their occupation of Britain more stretches of road were built, there are even traces and records of Roman roads as far away as Aberdeen in the North East of Scotland.

Every schoolboy is taught that the shortest distance between any two given points is a straight line and this was how the Romans set about building roads, arrow straight, as much as possible anyway, regardless of natural obstacles. These roads were built to provide an easy route

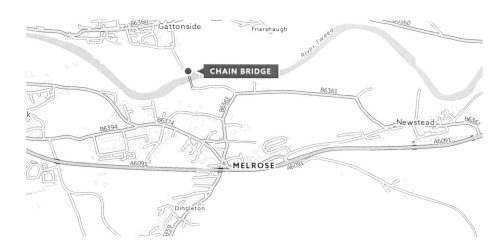

for men and supplies to be moved as quickly as possible to wherever they were needed, basically the motorways of their day. These vital supply links were guarded by a number of large super forts which were garrisoned by both foot soldiers and cavalry. In between these large forts and spaced at regular intervals were smaller forts with enough men stationed there to control normal day to day business. At the least sign of trouble however from local tribes these forts contacted each other using fire beacons lit at the top of their towers and very quickly reinforcements would be dispatched to quash any problems.

One of these super forts was erected at Trimontium an area close to Melrose. The name loosely translated means three hills which referred to the Eildon Hills immediately behind the fort. Trimontium would have housed over fifteen hundred troops and covered an area of fifteen acres. Surrounding that was a further partially fortified compound in excess of two hundred acres. This area housed the various businesses and support networks connected with the camps such as butchers, bakers, farmers, carpenters, fishermen, blacksmiths and many other trades. For such a large gathering of people there had of course to be accommodation, not just for the soldiers stationed there but also any patrols which were passing through and this would have been in the larger fortified area. The large number of people who were employed in the day to day running of such an extensive camp, either stayed at Trimontium or the villages nearby, The sheer scale of Trimontium can be appreciated by the fact that nearly two hundred drinking wells have been discovered in the region of the camp some going as deep as fifteen metres into the clay soil to locate drinking water for the inhabitants. These wells did not remain in use for ever and as the water supplies either dwindled or became unworkable, rather than have these open redundant wells situated all round the camps, the holes were filled with rubbish and eventually sealed off. The rubbish that the Romans filled these holes with, has of course been the equivalent to finding buried treasure to the archaeologists who have been working on the site. It is because of this rubbish and other items put in the out of use wells that so much of the everyday workings of Roman life in Britain can be pieced together. Trimontium is generally regarded as being the Head Quarters of the Roman Army in Scotland, a fact that is borne out by a Roman milestone found near Edinburgh, the distance inscribed on it being the distance to Trimontium. Another reason for surmising that Trimontium was indeed an important settlement is the discovery of an Amphitheatre in the area. This is the only Roman Amphitheatre discovered in Scotland and certainly the most northerly in the Roman Empire. An Amphitheatre would certainly have been a feature of a large settlement and amongst other things would have been used for weapons and combat training as well as an exercise and entertainment area for both troops and residents.

The Romans stayed in this area for over a hundred years and although references to Trimontium were made in Roman writings it had lain undiscovered until work began to construct a railway in the region in the early nineteenth century. It was during this work that remains were unearthed, and it was from this point onwards that the archaeologists involved discovered more and more remnants and were thus able to build a picture of what life was like in a Roman camp. Although the Romans withdrew from this area back to the defensive line of Hadrians Wall, they still very much had a controlling interest here and kept the local chieftans in line, either by bribing them with gifts or occasionally showing their military supremacy by sending raiding parties to quell any unrest. The Romans had during the course of building their Empire conquered many countries and it was from these countries that they drew recruits for their armies and navy. During the course of their service these recruits had seen the riches and potential of Britannia as it was then called and a few had even integrated with the local community. When the Romans finally withdrew from Trimontium many of these soldiers either deserted or left the service of the Roman military and stayed to become the new settlers and residents.

The Romans during the course of their occupation of Britain had built two massive defensive fortifications, Hadrian's Wall and The Antonine Wall. The latter is probably the least well known and lies across the waist of Scotland between the Firth of Clyde on the West coast and the Firth of Forth on the East coast and is roughly one hundred miles further north than Hadrians Wall. It is approximately forty miles long, ten feet high and fifteen feet wide and was constructed mainly of earth and stone. Building of the Antonine Wall began in 142AD and took approximately twelve years to build. The wall was the brainchild of Antoninus Pius who succeeded Hadrian, it is suggested that the wall may very well have been a vanity project by Antoninus as unlike Hadrian he had no military experience, no battle honours, and had never commanded a military force before becoming Emperor, he therefore needed something to enhance his image with the Roman public. This was the most northerly of the Roman defensive barriers and as well as the wall there was also a deep ditch on the Northern side. This ditch partly resulted from the removal of the earth and turf which had been dug to be used in the construction of the wall. The ditch though was very effective, as anybody attacking the wall had first to climb down into it to get to the base of the wall and this made them very vulnerable to attack from the troops stationed on the ramparts of the wall. At various points on both sides of the ditch the Romans had also dug holes called Lillias (Latin for lilies) as the holes were in the shape of lily petals, positioned in the holes were two sharpened pointed sticks (effectively the stamens of the flowers) the sticks were then coated with animal fat. These booby traps were then covered with grass and bracken and if the wall was being attacked it was more than likely that a number of the attackers would stumble into the holes especially if the attack was being carried out at night. Even a graze or a scratch from these pointed sticks was enough to make a wound turn septic and could even lead to death. On the South side of the wall a road had been built which allowed the fast transportation of men and supplies. There were at least sixteen forts guarding the length of the wall with several smaller forts in between. Despite the enormous expense, effort and manpower involved in building the wall it was more or less abandoned after only twenty years with the troops being relocated to the first and better known fortification line known as Hadrians Wall. The reason for its abandonment is not clear but the suggestion is that that it could have taken in the region of forty thousand men to guard the length of the wall and if the cost of supplying and maintaining this huge force was taken into consideration it was cheaper to bribe the local clan chiefs who were causing the Romans trouble than it was to maintain the defence of the wall. This theory has been somewhat verified by the discovery of a horde of silver Roman coins near the town of Falkirk on Scotland's east coast north of Edinburgh.

It is thought that construction of Hadrians Wall began in 122AD and took six years to complete, its height and width differs depending on the availability of construction materials but varies between twelve and twenty feet high with a similar variance in width. There was again a deep ditch on the Northern side similar to the Antonine wall and a military road on the Southern side. The ditches positioned on the Northern sides of both these walls resulted from digging out the earth to help form the wall but in so doing the Romans also made it much more difficult for anybody to attack the wall as they had to cross the ditch first thus presenting the defenders on the walls with an easy target. Both of these walls whilst initially thought of purely as a defensive barrier may have served a secondary purpose in that all traffic had to pass through gates positioned at various points along their length and it could therefore have been a way of controlling trade and extracting taxes and tolls from the people that used it. The wall was garrisoned by troops from countries conquered by the Romans and in effect it could be men from any of the countries which surrounded the Mediterranean Sea that had the task of guarding there most northerly frontier, with detachments of true Roman Legionaires in attendance for training purposes. It was not unknown for these men to desert the Roman Army and integrate with the local indigenous peoples. Troops from the Roman Empire continued to man the wall until the late 4th Century when the Roman administration and Legions began to leave Britain. It was gradually then left to local chieftans to administer and patrol. It is perhaps significant that in the whole of the Roman Empire which at that period involved most of Europe as we now know it and beyond, that there never was any record of constructions similar to either the Antonine or Hadrians wall. Was this because the various tribes of Northern England and Scotland caused the Romans so much trouble that they had to have a defensive line? or was it simply just a way to mark the extent of the lands they had conquered? There is no real answer to this question but either way as there are still extensive areas of wall remaining, after more than eighteen hundred years, it is surely a testament to the building prowess of the Romans.

The next significant mention in the history of Melrose was not until 631 AD when King Oswald of Northumbria invited Aidan of Iona (a saint in the making) to establish a monastery in Lindisfarne with a similar one to be constructed in Melrose. The intention being to try and convert the heathen Northumbrians to Christianity. It was some five hundred years later in 1136 that Melrose Abbey really became established. The construction of the Abbey as it is today took almost ten years to complete and it was built on a site not far from where the original abbey had stood. Over the next four hundred years until its destruction in 1544 the Cistercian monks who lived there, carried out their religious teachings not only in Melrose and the surrounding area but Scotland as a whole.

Unfortunately it seemed that Melrose Abbey was a very tempting prize and it was ransacked, burned, looted, and partially destroyed on various occasions. Its final demise came in 1544 when English armies were rampaging through many parts of Scotland. Melrose Abbey was so badly damaged at that time that it was never fully repaired although what was still standing managed to withstand one final assault from the troops of Oliver Cromwell as once again English armies invaded Scotland. The burial grounds round Melrose Abbey are said to contain the remains of King Alexander II of Scotland and a number of other members of the Scottish nobility, along with the embalmed heart of Robert the Bruce, the rest of his body being buried at Dunfermline Abbey. Melrose Abbey is open to the Public and it attracts thousands of tourists annually.

Situated within easy walking distance of the Abbey are two National Trust Scotland properties. The first of these is Priorwood Garden and Dried Flower Shop the name is a very significant clue as to what the shop sells, there is also however within the shop a drying room which is stocked with a vast range of flowers and you can wander round and pick your personal choice of blooms to order. Outside there is a new woodland area and an orchard which grows several historic apple varieties which could possibly be directly connected to the Abbey as it has been suggested that this area was the kitchen garden of the monks based at Melrose Abbey.

Harmony Garden is the other Trust property and was constructed at the beginning of the nineteenth century and considered by many to be the finest example of a Georgian Town house in Scotland. There is a walled garden measuring approximately three acres which feature lawns, flower and vegetable areas and a croquet lawn all within sight of the Abbey. The house is available to rent as a self catering holiday let as well as being host to the Borders Book Festival which is an annual event usually held in June.

I am sure it would be considered sacrilege by many if I were to leave Melrose without mentioning what is probably the largest spectator sport in the Borders, that sport being Rugby. Virtually every town of any significant size in the Borders has a rugby team, sometimes even two or more and it is very much part of the curriculum in schools at both junior and senior levels. Football, is also played and there are a few Borders towns which have football teams but they do not have anything like the fan base which the Rugby Clubs attract. There are no large clusters of population in the Borders, no cities that attract hordes of people to live in them so it is perhaps surprising that from a relatively sparsely populated area so many people indulge in this one particular sport, either as players or spectators.

It is Rugby Union that is practiced in this region, one of the two codes of the game, the other being Rugby League. In Rugby Union there are fifteen players per side who play on a pitch one hundred metres long by seventy metres wide with H-shaped goal posts at either

MELROSE ABBEY

THE GREENYARDS RUGBY GROUND, MELROSE

end. Given that the game is so popular here in the Borders, it is perhaps a surprise that this is not where the game of Rugby started. That particular accolade goes to a town in middle England called funnily enough, Rugby, and it was at Rugby School in 1823, so the story goes that a certain William Webb Ellis who was a pupil there picked up the ball whilst playing a game similar to football and ran with it, and so the game of Rugby was born.

The trophy which is awarded to the winners of the Rugby World Cup is in fact called the Webb Ellis Cup and has been previously won by Australia, South Africa New Zealand and England. The current holders (at time of writing) are New Zealand who had a narrow victory over France in 2011.

I am not going to attempt here, to try and explain the rules of rugby, suffice to say that when you have thirty men on a pitch attempting to get their hands on one ball and score points by reaching the opponents goal posts, it can get very, shall we say interesting and exciting. A large part of the game of Rugby is as you can imagine, physical, and it is very much a contact sport. Some of the players can be one hundred kilos plus and it takes a very brave man to attempt to stop an opponent of that size thundering down the pitch, ball in hand towards you. Is it the fresh air, the good food, or being descended from tough farming stock that produce men with the necessary physique to qualify as players here in the Borders? I don't think anybody really has the answer to that question but, whatever it is, long may it continue.

The very first International Game of Rugby was played on the 27th March 1871 between surprise, surprise, England and Scotland, which I am pleased to say Scotland won, but by the narrowest of margins. It is ironic perhaps that the English and Scots who had been fighting, murdering, and stealing from each other for longer than anyone can remember, then organize a so called "friendly" competition in what is classed as a full contact sport and played between the two oldest enemies in the world. The game of Rugby was initially classed rightly or wrongly as a gentleman's sport and was always played on an amateur basis. However as its popularity grew then so did the potential for advertisers and investors to make money and it was in 1995 that the game was "opened up" and players were allowed to receive payment. This of course then meant sponsorship, television, and the buying in of players from other teams and indeed even other countries as the game of Rugby had now become a global sport. The Greenyards is the home pitch for Melrose Rugby Football Club and it was here in 1883 that Ned Haig a butcher by profession and a Melrose player thought of a new version of rugby, an idea which would revolutionize the game of rugby and make it more attractive to an even bigger worldwide audience.

The Melrose Club were apparently suffering some financial problems at that time and ideas were being discussed as to how they could raise money to replenish their coffers. The idea of a knockout tournament involving several teams was suggested, however as each normal game of rugby was played for at least eighty minutes it would not be possible to fit all the matches into a one day event. It was then that Ned Haig came up with a revolutionary proposal which would involve cutting the teams back from fifteen players each side to just seven and cutting the playing time to seven minutes each half with a one minute half time break. The new "sevens" game would still be played on a full size pitch and the rules and scoring would also stay the same. It would however, require a different style of play and indeed player. The game was now much faster, it also meant players had to be more adaptable, scrums and lineouts would only involve six players, three players from each side instead of sixteen or so previously. The ball was never trapped under a pile of bodies but was quickly fed out to the fast moving "backs" and it became more of a running game.

The first Melrose "sports" day featuring this new style of rugby was held in April 1883, and included as well as rugby, foot races and other athletic events. The rational behind having various other sports included was I suppose to appeal to as wide an audience as possible as it was not known how this new concept of the game of rugby would be accepted by the die hard fans who had previously only known the traditional game of rugby, and even if they would accept it at all. However there was no need to worry, it was a great success and the idea very quickly spread to other clubs in the area. It has continued to grow ever since. Sevens tournaments now take place world wide, including Africa, America, Asia, Europe and of course the Southern Hemisphere countries. 'Sevens' has now even been recognized as an Olympic Sport and the first competition will be in the Summer Olympics of 2016. The game of rugby and in particular "sevens" have indeed come a long, long way from the initial idea designed to provide a little extra financial funding for the bank account of a struggling local rugby club.

CHAPTER 9

newstead, leaderfoot viaduct, border reivers dryburgh abbey

Very close to Melrose lies the village of Newstead, its claim to fame being that it is recognized as being the oldest continually inhabited village in Scotland. This statement could very well be true as Newstead has links all the way back to when the Romans were at Trimontium. Because of its proximity to Melrose it was also the place where builders, tradesmen and other workers stayed while construction programmes such as Melrose Abbey were being undertaken. More recently it was home to workers who in 1865 were constructing the Leaderfoot Railway Viaduct, which we will talk about in more detail shortly.

On the other side of the River Tweed less than a mile away from Melrose is a village called Gattonside. The origin of the name has not been fully discovered but it has distinct connections with Melrose in that in 1143 the lands of Gattonside were granted to the monks of Melrose Abbey by King David 1st of Scotland. It was prime agricultural land and the monks had a number of orchards there which they farmed. There is no direct road link from Gattonside to Melrose, although a road connection that involves travelling several miles in either direction from Gattonside to reach Melrose is available. When the monks farmed the orchards they crossed the Tweed using a ford, carrying the produce across with them. Much

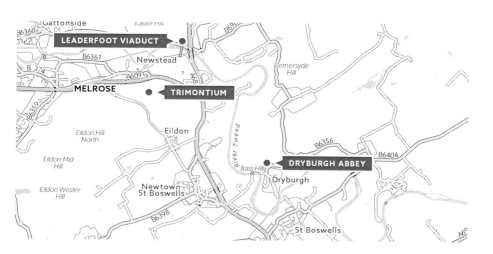

RIVER TWEED, MELROSE

THE IMPOSING LEADERFOOT VIADUCT

later in 1826 the Gattonside Suspension Bridge was built, known locally as the Chain Bridge, it is still in use today and is for the use of pedestrians only.

Just over two miles downstream from Melrose is Leaderfoot Viaduct. This viaduct carried a single track railway line from Reston on the East Coast main line to St. Boswells on the Waverley Line, over the River Tweed. It was opened in 1865 and is composed of nineteen arches each with a span of forty three feet and at its highest point is one hundred and twenty feet above the river Tweed. Leaderfoot is where the River Leader joins the Tweed and is also the site of two other bridges, both road bridges. Whilst the Viaduct is very impressive the original Drygrange Bridge carrying the A68 main road from the South towards Edinburgh which was built in 1779 has a central span of thirty one metres, an enormous construction span for that period. This road is now closed to motorised traffic, but is still open to pedestrians. It was replaced by a wider, more modern bridge in 1971 which now carries all the vehicular traffic. The railway was severed in 1948 due to flooding and was never again used for passenger traffic although goods trains still used the line up until 1965. The condition of the Viaduct bridge gradually deteriorated through non use. Until in1991 when under threat of demolition, remedial work was carried out. The repairs took over a year, as work quite often had to be stopped due to adverse weather, in particular strong winds, which made trying to repair brickwork from a bosuns chair swaying one hundred plus feet above the ground extremely difficult.

We have at this point on our journey following the course of the River Tweed travelled more or less halfway and during the telling of the story so far the Border Reivers have been mentioned more than once. It would seem therefore to be a good time to explain in more detail who and what they were. First of all forget any romantic ideals or notions you may have in your mind of people righting wrongs and helping the poor "Robin Hood" style, this is the image of Reivers generally portrayed in fictional stories and even perhaps in some of the Border ballads and poems. In reality though think instead of cattle and sheep rustling, kidnapping, extortion, protection money, blood feuds and ruthless revenge raids, which, no doubt could very well be the basis for the script of a Hollywood movie. Incidentally, as we have mentioned films, I would like at this juncture to tell you that the Border Scots, did not wear kilts, this was a clothing style more associated with the inhabitants of the Highlands. They did not paint their faces blue or shout "freedom" at every given opportunity, This is Mel Gibson's purely fictional portrayal of the Scots and was done no doubt to look better on the big screens and of course for financial reasons also, but the story he portrayed was generally inaccurate throughout. Truth, in fact however, lets face it was never the basis for any good film. All the misdemeanors nevertheless which I mentioned at the beginning of this chapter did occur on a regular basis, this was the lawless nature of the Scottish Border Country from the late 13th Century to the early 17th Century.

They (the Reivers) were not one organized group, but instead were several bands of bloodthirsty individuals loosely family or clan connected. They would quite happily fight with or against anybody, it has even been noted that on at least one occasion a group of Border Reivers swopped sides during the course of a battle in order to be on the winning side. It is also widely thought that Reivers only existed on the Scottish side of the Border but in fact they were prevalent on the English side as well. Many family surnames or variations of that name existed on both sides of the Border and whilst it was not common and indeed it was frowned upon and forcibly discouraged there were instances of members of opposing families being romantically connected. The Reivers came into being as a result of almost constant wars and feuds in this area. The law, or at least, the ability of someone to uphold the law was virtually non-existent. As a result these groups made their own rules and regulations (Border Law) these self made laws by the resident families of the Borders Region were basically designed for self preservation. It is generally recognized that the words "blackmail" and "bereavement" in the English language came about as a direct result of Reiver activities on both sides of the Border. No mercy was asked for and very rarely, if at all, was it given. One other factor in the Reivers emergence was a border law which stated that a man's land and estate had to be divided between his sons, on his death. The result of this law was that estates and land were split into ever smaller packages through the generations and there were many families who had insufficient land to provide an income to support themselves and whilst not attempting to justify it, or give them an excuse to murder and rob, they had to find an alternative source of income, and this quite often was achieved through reiving or livestock rustling.

Reiving was not only confined to the lower classes either, many landowners and nobility also took an active part in it. In fact the Wardens of the Marches (effectively governors of defined land areas) who were supposed to enforce the few laws which were in existence, were often as bad if not worse than those they were supposed to govern. Even if the supposed law enforcers did not participate in the actual raids themselves, they would receive a sizeable part of the proceeds from these raids. By effectively turning a blind eye to what was happening, these supposed law enforcers only encouraged further law breaking and the vicious spiral continued unchecked.

Much of the Border country was unsuitable for arable farming, as has been mentioned previously, whilst not necessarily mountainous, it was certainly hilly with large tracts of wood or moorland. This type of terrain though, was ideal for grazing cattle, sheep and horses. It was also the perfect environment for the Reivers. Livestock could easily be appropriated, especially by lightly mounted horsemen who knew the area. As a bonus, if they managed to capture individuals who were then able to be held to ransom, it could and often did become a very profitable evenings work. Reading about the Reivers so far you may well be asking yourself how and why such lawlessness was allowed to exist. Why was the law which was applicable in other areas of Britain not being enforced in the Borders?. Why was nothing being done to prevent these kind of outrages occurring in the first place? The answer was fairly straightforward. The governments of both England and Scotland were prepared, it seemed to tolerate the lawlessness, that was happening in the Border counties, up to a certain point. It was after all, these fierce fighting border men who were the first line of defence against invading forces from either side. However it would appear to be the case, that every now and then, if the offences that these groups committed reached an intolerable level, the respective governments would react. People would be arrested, often indiscriminately and prosecuted in a rather draconian fashion, no doubt to try and dissuade others from committing similar outrages, crimes and violations, in the future.

The "season" for Reiving tended to be in the winter when nights were long and dark, cattle, sheep and horses were fat and healthy after a summer of grazing and perhaps more importantly they were all grouped together. The Reivers usually kept their raids to within a days ride of their base. Although Northumbrian Reivers have been known to have raided as far North as Edinburgh, whilst their Scottish counterparts were known to have raided as far South as Yorkshire. The raiding groups varied in size from a dozen or so men up to what could be classed as a small army of perhaps a hundred or so men. The success of these raids depended on surprise, swiftness and agility, therefore the Reivers wore very little in the way of armour and carried only light weapons. They were regarded by many as being the best light cavalry force in Europe. Reivers were often recruited as mercenaries for various Scottish and English wars. Some were even forced to join either the Scottish or English armies after being convicted of a heinous crime, the statutory penalty for which was death. The death sentence would then be suspended if they enlisted and agreed to take part in whichever conflict was being fought at that particular time. It was also not unknown for this particular sentence to be applied to the perpetrator's sons as well.

It seems strange in amongst all this crime and lawlessness where your very existence quite often hung by a very fine thread, that there was it would seem codes of chivalry and one of these in particular is somewhat surprising. Even in times of relative peace there was always a certain amount of tension between the peoples living on either side of the Border and because of this laws exclusive only to the Borders came into being. One of these laws in particular stated that if your property was raided, you had the right within six days to mount a counter raid to recover your property even if this meant crossing the Border. In such raids the family that were the "victims" were required to let people know what was happening and were required to announce their intentions by carrying a burning turf on the point of a spear and to make a noise with "hounds and horn" this was supposedly to distinquish themselves from the standard "run of the mill" illegal raiding party. Anybody who met or was caught up in one of these "legal" raids was required to ride along and help as much as possible or otherwise be considered as being compliant with the original illegal raiders. It certainly appears these days anyway to be a strange way to uphold the law and provide justice for Border residents.

The late 16th Century and early 17th Century was the period in history when the Reivers were at their strongest, a time when the Tudors were dominant in England and the Stuart Kings controlled Scotland. At the time of the death of Elizabeth the 1st in 1603, the situation in the Borders was so bad that the English Government was even considering the possibility of re-building and manning Hadrians Wall. It had become especially violent because of the convenient belief of the Reivers that all laws were suspended on the death of a Monarch and only came into being again when their successor was appointed. There was therefore a period of approximately a week (Ill Week) after Elizabeth the 1st's death when for want of a better expression all hell was let loose in the Borders and raids, death and destruction were carried out on both sides of the Border completely unchecked and on a monumental scale. The new Monarch, in this instance, the successor to Queen Elizabeth was of course James V1 of Scotland, James 1st of England, the first King of a united England and Scotland. Upon his appointment as King he decided to act against the rebellious Borderers. The Border families had no love for James, whom they regarded as being more English than Scots and someone who was more interested in personal achievement rather than the welfare of his subjects. James, very soon after his coronation came down hard on the activities of the Border Reivers. Border Law was abolished as was the "Borders" as a name and it was replaced with the name "Middle Shires." These new laws and the crackdown on violence in effect meant the beginning of the end for the Reivers and the way they had existed for centuries beforehand..

The main Border towns have during the summer months a festival week which has a direct link back to the Reivers. The "Borders Common Ridings" are an annual event which commemorates the lawlessness of the Reiving era. Not only did the Reivers make cross border raids and steal from the English, they were not averse to stealing from their own neighbours either. Whilst this was mainly cattle and livestock, basically anything that had any value and was portable was at risk. The land boundaries of each clan or community were usually marked with large stones or boulders, but a group of strong men could move these stones and make their family's territory larger and so it was that regular inspections were made to make sure that neighbours had not encroached upon your land. The chief or leader of any particular clan or community would appoint a prominent local townsperson to "Ride The Marches" or boundaries of their territory and make sure that everything was as it should be. Even when relative peace was restored to the Borders and these ride outs were not deemed necessary they continued as a way of remembering history and tradition. These celebrations continue even today and most of the Border Towns appoint a young man usually in early spring as the representative of their town, he is generally accompanied by a young lady and several principal attendants. Together they carry out a number of official ceremonies during the course of the year. Their main duties take place over a period of roughly a week when their particular town has its own "Common Riding" The two principals are accompanied on horseback by several main attendants and what can amount to several hundred followers all on horseback. Although nowadays whilst there is still a certain amount of historical fact connected with the ceremonies and events which are performed at various points on the route, it has more of a carnival atmosphere, and the crowds of people who turn out to watch the cavalcade are in a party mood. The people watching and cheering the celebrations are not just the local townspeople, they are ex-pats and tourists from all over the world as well as many visitors from the rest of the Borders region. The sight and sound of several hundred horses being ridden through the streets is enough to set most hearts racing. Each town's principal "Lad and Lass" carry the colours of their community, normally the town flag. The colours are "bussed" which symbolises the days when knights would ask ladies to tie their coloured ribbons to their lances or spears as a good luck token when he was going to battle. Each town's representatives also take part in the ceremonies of their neighbouring towns and it means that the summer months in the Borders can have very much a party atmosphere with all manner of events taking place. Traditionally Hawick starts these celebrations usually in the first week of June and the other border towns follow on

DRYBURGH ABBEY

from that, which means that for about three or four months there is a least one border town having a celebration, a far cry indeed from what it commemorates.

Dryburgh Abbey, a short distance downstream from Leaderfoot was founded in 1150. The Abbey was attacked and set alight by English troops in 1322. After being restored, it once again suffered a similar fate when English troops attacked it again in 1385. After being restored once more the Abbey enjoyed a period of relative calm and prosperity until finally it was destroyed in 1544 by Richard the 2nd. Dryburgh Abbey never seemed to have the patronage or the income that other abbeys in the area such as Melrose and Kelso enjoyed. Consequently repair work and increasing the size of the Abbey was always delayed due to lack of funds. The monks at Dryburgh were of the Premonostratensian Order founded by Saint Norbert of Xanten, they followed a very austere monastic life and wore white habits. The Abbey managed to continue with help from various donors but was never able to reach the financial highs enjoyed by its neighbouring abbeys and by 1600 all its monks had died, through natural causes, which effectively meant the end of the Abbey. By 1604 all the lands and possessions of the Abbey were integrated into The Lordship of Cardross. Dryburgh Abbey is the burial place of Sir Walter Scott, also Field-Marshall Earl Haig, who commanded the British Army during the First World War and the Earl of Buchan.

DRYBURGH ABBEY

scott's view, bemersyde house, st. boshells, mertoun house, jedburgh, mary, queen of scots

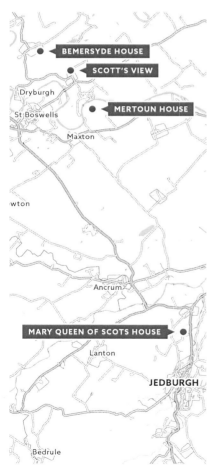

BEMERSYDE HOUSE

SCOTT'S VIEW

Dryburgh

MERTOUN HOUSE

St Boswells

Maxton

wton

Ancrum

MARY QUEEN OF SCOTS HOUSE

Lanton

JEDBURGH

Bedrule

There are several places of interest close to Dryburgh Abbey including Scott's View, named after Sir Walter Scott, which offers a breathtaking view of the Borders countryside. The Wallace Monument which stands in the grounds of Bemersyde House and is a tribute to Sir William Wallace, who as a patriot of Scotland fought many battles against the English during the course of the 13th Century. The statue was commissioned by the 11th Earl of Buchan David Stuart Erskine and stands a massive thirty one feet high. It was unveiled in 1814 and renovated in 1991. The years and the weather having taken their toll of the red sandstone from which it is made. Bemersyde House itself dates back as far as 1535 when originally it was a Peel Tower, these were fortified structures which were built mainly along the line of the Tweed Valley although there are similar structures in other parts of the country. They were originally designed as lookout towers and by an Act of Parliament in 1455 had to have an iron basket on their roofs capable of containing a fire which could be lit if there was any danger. This warning signal could then be seen by either the next tower or castle and the local populace would take refuge until the danger had passed. Bemersyde House was bought by the British Government in 1921 and

WILLIAM WALLACE MONUMENT

SCOTT'S VIEW AND EILDON HILLS, WITH RIVER TWEED JUST VISIBLE IN THE FOREGROUND

given to Field Marshall Douglas Haig The 1st Earl Haig as a gift in recognition of his endeavours in commanding the British Forces during the First World War. The original tower has been extended and it is now a sizeable country house with extensive gardens which are open to the public during the summer months.

The village of St. Boswells is nearby and is named after Saint Boisil who was an abbot at Melrose Abbey. St. Boswells sits astride St Cuthbert's Way a long distance walkway which stretches from Melrose Abbey to the Holy Island of Lindisfarne situated just off the Northumbrian Coast of England a distance of sixty two miles through beautiful countryside both North and South of the Border. It does seem a fitting and worthwhile reminder that the two areas are linked in this way as it was monks from Lindisfarne who began the building of Melrose Abbey in their attempt to spread Christianity throughout Scotland and the Borders region in particular.

Mertoun House is situated less than four kilometres (two miles) East of St. Boswells virtually on the banks of the River Tweed and is currently the home of The 7th Duke of Sutherland. Mertoun House is Category "A" listed as is the dovecote adjacent to the house which dates back to the 16th Century. Dovecotes were an integral part of grand houses during that period, they could either be round or square, attached to or separate from the main house. They were built with holes in the walls to provide nesting sites and a roost for pigeons and doves. The pigeons were an essential alternative supply of fresh meat, eggs and also fertilizer for the gardens. In 1984 The Mertoun Gardens Trust was established by the Duke to look after the twenty six acres of gardens attached to the house and these are now open to the public.

One of the main roads linking Scotland and England, the A68, virtually passes through St. Boswells and if you continue south from St. Boswells on the A68 for approximately ten miles you will arrive at Jedburgh. This is one of the places which again whilst it is not directly linked to the Tweed has so much history within its walls it would be difficult to exclude it entirely from a Borders life story.

Jedburgh sits on the Jed Water a tributary of the River Teviot which in turn is a tributary of the River Tweed so I suppose there is a faint connection involved, however Jedburgh is famous in it's own right. Buildings of note in Jedburgh are the ruins of Jedburgh Abbey and Jedburgh Castle, there is also the house once lived in by Mary Queen of Scots and Jedburgh Castle jail. As it is positioned only ten miles from the Border, and if you have read the previous few chapters you will appreciate that Jedburgh suffered greatly in the Border wars and skirmishes and was as often in English hands as it was Scots. The town is dominated by the ruins of Jedburgh Abbey which was started as a priory in 1138 by monks from the Augustinian Order who arrived here from France. The priory was elevated to the status of an Abbey in 1154. The streets of Jedburgh have been walked along by many famous people including Sir Walter Scott, William Wordsworth, Robert Burns and Bonnie Prince Charlie. There is also on the outskirts of Jedburgh a house which is thought to have been lived in by Mary Queen of Scot's for a short time in 1566. Mary had what can be best described as a rather eventful life. She acceded to the Scottish throne at the tender age of six days when her father King James V died. Because of her age Scotland was ruled by Regents and they had reached an agreement with King Henry II of France that Mary would marry his son Dauphin Francois in return for military and financial help in the fight against their common enemy, England. Mary was moved to France for her own protection when King Henry VIII invaded Scotland to try and force Mary to marry his son the future King Edward II. Mary spent her childhood at the French Court and did indeed marry Francois only for tragedy to strike less than a year later when he died from a serious illness. Within a year the still grief stricken Mary had left France and returned to Scotland to claim her throne. It was not the happiest of homecomings, Mary was a staunch Roman Catholic and there were several Protestant Lords in positions of power in the Scottish government which inevitably led to arguments and dissent.

Mary renewed her friendship with Henry Stewart, Lord Darnley, whom she married in 1565. Lord Darnley was a fairly ambitious person and he was not content with only being King Consort. He wanted Mary to sanction his proposal for equal status so that in the event of her dying before him he would become King, Mary refused to agree to this proposal and he could see that his hopes might never be realized. He became extremely jealous of Mary's private

MARY QUEEN OF SCOT'S HOUSE, JEDBURGH

secretary who he considered might even be having an affair with her. This jealousy reached such an extent that he led a group of armed men who murdered the secretary in front of the then pregnant Mary. Inevitably this put a severe strain on their marriage and in the early part of 1567 Darnley mysteriously died in an explosion which destroyed the house he was staying in whilst recovering from an illness. One of the chief suspects for Darnley's death was the Earl of Bothwell, whom it was rumoured was having an affair with Mary, he was tried but found not guilty of Darnley's death. What led to further speculation however was that Mary and Bothwell then married within one month of his acquittal. It was not a popular wedding in Scotland and led to an uprising in which Bothwell was exiled and Mary was held prisoner in Loch Leven Castle. At this point she was forced to abdicate in favour of James her one year old son fathered by Darnley. Mary escaped from Loch Leven and tried unsuccessfully to regain the throne at which point she fled to England to seek protection from Queen Elizabeth I who regarded Mary as a threat to her and her sovereignty and promptly imprisoned Mary in various castles throughout England for the next eighteen years. In her nineteenth year of imprisonment Mary was accused of treason, found guilty and subsequently beheaded at Fotheringhay Castle in February 1587, the final event in a tempestuous life.

Jedburgh is known locally as "Jethart" and "Jethart Justice" was in fact anything but that. It is reported that a gang of villains had been captured in Jedburgh, the crime for which they were arrested and supposed to have committed is not mentioned. They were then, within a very short time of being arrested, found guilty, sentenced and summarily executed straight away, without a fair and proper trial. It is suggested that a trial may have been held after the event but whether it was, or it wasn't would not have done these poor particular individuals any good. Whether justice such as this, occurred only in this one instance, or was carried out on a regular basis is open to speculation but is part of the myths that make history interesting. Jedburgh Castle was fought over and damaged so many times that it was demolished as early as 1409 by Sir James Douglas of Balvenie. The site was later to become Jedburgh Castle Jail and is now a museum, complete with resident ghosts and presentations to show what life as a prisoner was like in the early 19th century. It was also recently featured on British national television and portrayed as being one of the ghostliest places in Britain. Less than two miles (three kilometres) from the centre of Jedburgh and close to the main A68 route between England and Scotland is one of the oldest trees in the United Kingdom. "The Capon Oak" is thought to be in the region of one thousand years old and its name is derived from the Capuchin monks who it is said rested under its branches whilst traveling to and from Jedburgh Abbey. Despite the trunk being split in two and having to be supported, the tree is still actually growing and has a girth at its base of nearly thirty three feet (ten metres) The oak is one of the top fifty trees in the U.K. which were selected to mark Her Majesty Queen Elizabeth's Golden Jubilee. The trees selected to make up these top fifty are either famous through history or legend, extremely old, ancient or large and the Capon Oak ranks alongside the "Fortingall Yew" which is also in Scotland, and with estimates of its age being between three thousand and five thousand years, is supposedly the oldest living organism in Europe.

JEDBURGH CASTLE

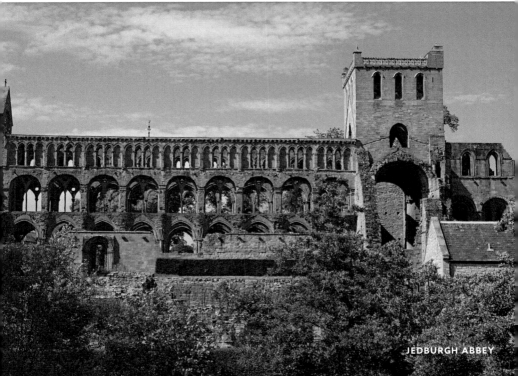

JEDBURGH ABBEY

FLOORS CASTLE NEAR KELSO

CHAPTER 11

roxburgh, floors castle, kelso, coldstream

Having completed our "off piste" visit to Jedburgh our journey down the River Tweed continues and passes close to Roxburgh. The current village of Roxburgh is some two miles South West of the historic Roxburgh which held a very strategic position on a peninsula between the Rivers Tweed and Teviot. A castle was built there on the narrowest part of the peninsula and it therefore became a target for numerous raids. Roxburgh was classed as being as important as the cities of Edinburgh, Perth or Stirling and was in fact for some time the Royal residence of King David the First of Scotland. Part of its importance also seems to have arisen from its position on the banks of the Tweed and its proximity to Berwick, which allowed access to the port and the North Sea, via the River Tweed. Whilst doing research into the river however, it was suggested that the Tweed was not navigable for craft of any significant size after only a few miles inland from the estuary so this particular point of importance for Roxburgh is very much in question.

Roxburgh because of its importance and Royal connections was constantly under attack and changed hands several times. It's final capture in 1460 saw the castle and the village virtually destroyed. It's importance was also lessened by the English capture of Berwick-on-Tweed in 1482 which made any river access that it may have had unimportant and the village and castle ceased to exist apart from a few ruins.

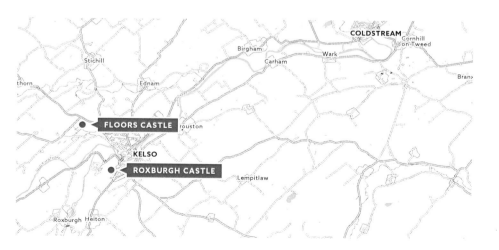

Looking North across the River Tweed from the ancient site of Roxburgh, Floors Castle is visible, more a grand country home, than a military building as the name would suggest. It is however classified as the largest inhabited castle in Scotland and is the residence of the Duke and Duchess of Roxburghe and their family. Originally built in the 1720's it's name is thought to be derived from Scotland's old alliance with France and the French word for flowers (fleurs). It may also have come from the fact that the building was constructed on "floors" or terraces. The lands round Floors were controlled by the monks of Kelso Abbey until the time of the Reformation at which point James V1 gave the lands to Robert Ker who was later to become the 1st Earl of Roxburghe. It was when the 5th Earl, who played an important part in the Union of Scotland and England in 1707, was rewarded by being made the first Duke of Roxburghe that he commissioned William Adam to redesign Floors. This work took five years to complete and was done between 1721 and 1726 consisting of one main central block with symmetrical buildings either side which were the stables, kitchens and servants quarters. The building was again re-modelled around 1837 by architect William Playfair and the current building is the result of his work. You may think when you see Floors Castle that it seems to be vaguely familiar and this will be most likely if you are a film fan as Floors Castle was the setting for the 1984 film "Greystoke" "Legend of Tarzan, Lord of the Apes." As has previously been mentioned regarding so many of the other great country houses we have visited, the cost of maintaining a building and grounds of this size

MARKET SQUARE, KELSO

KELSO ABBEY

is enormous and as a result therefore Floors Castle is open to the public. Not only the house but also extensive grounds, a restaurant and a garden centre where plants grown on the estate along with a host of other items can be purchased.

Only minutes away from Floors castle is the town of Kelso, which sits where the River Teviot joins the Tweed. Kelso was no more than a hamlet until the arrival of monks to Kelso Abbey in 1128. Many of the monks were skilled craftsmen and it was their expertise and guidance which helped Kelso to expand rapidly and become one of the Borders' richest towns, this continued for many years despite the various attacks which the Abbey suffered and it was only when the Reformation occurred in the 16th Century and the Abbey had less control over the grounds and area in which it was situated that growth slowed down. The ruins of Kelso Abbey are only a short walk from the centre and open to the public, well worth a visit if only just to admire the skills required to build such a structure.

There are two main bridges in Kelso which span the Tweed, the oldest of the two being Rennie's Bridge which was built in 1803 by John Rennie, who later went on to build the Waterloo Bridge in London. His bridge in Kelso was the scene of riots in 1854 after the local population objected to tolls still being charged to use the bridge long after the building costs were covered. This led to the "Riot Act" being read by the local peace keepers. This was a law in force at that time which allowed the local authorities to deal with groups of troublemakers consisting of twelve or more people, deemed to be causing a disturbance or public nuisance. It has to be pointed out however that shortly after this disturbance, the tolls were abolished. Less than a mile downstream is the second more modern bridge which was designed and constructed to take today's heavier vehicular traffic away from the town. Kelso is recognized as having the largest town market square in Scotland. If that isn't enough to warrant a mention into the record books then the fact that the square is still cobbled, as are the four streets which guide you into the square, will certainly make you remember it as you shake and vibrate your way across. If you do stop and browse around the shops in the square, (very much recommended), you will find that there are a large number of independent, artisan businesses, as well as small friendly cafes. With plenty of seating areas situated in the square and masses of flowers decorating the surrounding buildings especially during the summer months, you can while away the time and enjoy a coffee whilst peacefully watching the world pass by.

Kelso has at least one other claim to fame and that is its racecourse. The first recorded race at Kelso was in 1734, but racing at the current course venue started in 1822 and was flat racing until 1888 and since then has adopted The National Hunt rules. The official website for the course describes itself as " The Friendliest Racecourse in Britain" and in 2007 was voted the best small racecourse in Scotland and Northern England.

Back to the riverbank and our journey downstream continues until we reach

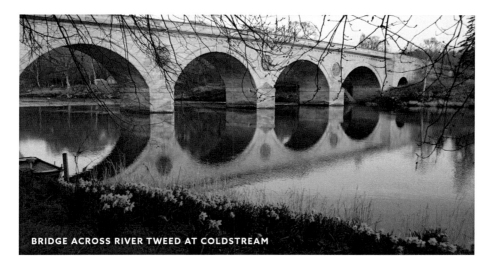

BRIDGE ACROSS RIVER TWEED AT COLDSTREAM

Coldstream, which is a small town situated on the north bank of the Tweed. The South bank being Northumberland and England, the river Tweed at this point really does constitute the Border between England and Scotland. Coldstream is a former burgh town which meant that a portion of the laws and administration for the town could be done locally rather than through the National Government. After changes in the Local Government re-organisation of 1975 however, whilst the Burgh name remained for Coldstream and many other towns it was purely ceremonial and served no real purpose with respect to administration. Coldstream lends its name however to perhaps one of the most famous regiments in the British Army, The Coldstream Guards.

The regiment was formed in 1650 by General George Monck. after he asked for and was then given, permission by Oliver Cromwell to do so. Within a few weeks of forming his new regiment, he was in action at the Battle of Dunbar, where the Roundheads defeated the forces of Charles Stuart. Monck's regiment was then stationed in Scotland as a deterrent against any further troubles. When Cromwell abdicated, Monck gathered his forces together and crossed The Tweed at Coldstream. He then began marching his men towards London and finally arrived there nearly five weeks later in February 1660.

The new government had ordered the disbanding of all regiments previously linked to Cromwell's New Model Army but because of Monck's help and loyalty they, (the regiment) were immediately asked to take up arms again as The Lord General's Regiment of Foot Guards. It was when Monck died in 1670 and The Earl of Craven took command of the Regiment that it was re-named, The Coldstream Regiment of Foot Guards. It was not until

1855 that their name was finally changed to The Coldstream Guards and since then they have been deployed in virtually every theatre of war that has had British involvement right up to the present day including Iraq, Afghanistan, Bosnia and Ireland. The times when the public are most likely to see the members of this famous regiment in their very distinctive uniforms is during the course of ceremonial parades in London including the Queen's Birthday Parade, Opening of Parliament, Trooping the Colour and Rememberance Sunday. Athough they are based in Scotland they consider themselves to be very much an English Regiment with their recruitment area being mostly in the North East of England.

During the 18th and 19th centuries Coldstream was a popular venue for runaway marriages almost as popular as Gretna Green is at present. One of Britains former Prime Ministers Sir Alec Douglas Home who served from 1963 to 1964 is buried at Coldstream, the Home family having extensive family estates in the locality.

There is one other great game besides Rugby, which is played in the Borders and that game is golf. Close to Coldstream is Hirsel Golf Club which is featured in Golf Monthly's hundred hidden gems of the U.K. and Ireland. The better known golf courses of Scotland tend to be situated further North in The Lothians , Fife or even The Highlands. It is because they are anxious to get to these courses that golfers quite often pass through the Borders sometimes even without stopping. In lots of respects this is a shame and a pity as there are many fine courses scattered all along the Border Counties, at least twenty one at the last count with all tastes and abilities catered for. There are championship courses at Roxburghe and Cardrona (known as the Gleneagles of the South) and the Borders only coastal course at Eyemouth where the par three sixth hole is actually played across a gully with the North Sea waves crashing below. However I am sure that the local members of clubs such as Hirsel, which is an eighteen hole par seventy course, and has been referred to as The Augusta of the North, are very appreciative of the fact that they do not have to compete with hosts of visitors when trying to book a round. Whilst the course is set in open parkland it has all the required necessary hazards including woodland, thick shrubbery, water features and a sometimes very fierce rough. There are several of the eighteen holes that require blind tee shots and if that initial tee shot is a little wayward, off line or short, it could be that the second shot also requires to be taken blind. Just to make things even more attractive for golfers either living in the Borders or passing through is the "Freedom of the Fairways" scheme which allows upon purchase of a "passport" access to a considerable number of golf courses with apart from a few restrictions almost unlimited availability.

SALMON FISHERMAN ON RIVER TWEED AT KELSO.

battle of flodden, jim clark

DUNS

JIM CLARK MUSEUM

Edrom

Allanton

Whitsome

Horndea

Swinton

Ladykirk   Nor

Leitholm

Donaldson's
Lodge

Lennel

COLDSTREAM

Birgham   Cornhill
                   on Tweed
          Wark
Carham

Branxton

SITE OF THE BATTLE OF FLODDEN

I have made several references in previous pages to the losses suffered by Border towns and villages in the Battle of Flodden. This battle took place near Coldstream, at a village called Branxton in Northumberland in September 1513. The main combatants were once again the Scots and the English. The Scots were under the command of King James IVth and the English were under the command of The Earl of Surrey. This was because the English Monarch, King Henry VIII was involved at that time in another dispute - ie a war with France. It was because of this war and "The Auld Alliance" between France and Scotland that King Louis XII of France had asked King James to invade England to try and divert some of Henry's troops away from France. In theory this was a good idea but in practice Henry had recruited his French invasion force from mainly the Southern Counties of Britain, leaving The Earl of Surrey, Henry's right hand man to recruit an army from the Northern Counties, ready to meet the Scottish invasion threat.

Codes of chivalry once again came into play in the run up to this battle and James had actually given the English one month's notice of his intention to invade, which allowed the English plenty of time to muster an army and prepare for battle. In terms of actual physical troop numbers it was the biggest battle ever fought between the two countries. Reports suggest that the Scots had an army of 30,000, whilst the English army was approximately 20,000. In most historical accounts there is a margin of error and various reports give details of many desertions from the Scottish army during its long march to Flodden. Regardless of these reports this was indeed a big battle. The Scots made a number of basic mistakes which had a significant effect on the outcome of the battle. When English troops were spotted in a vulnerable position trying to perform an outflanking manouevre King James refused to allow artillery to be re-positioned and used against them as this was deemed to be ungentlemanly. Because of these codes of ethics and chivalry this allowed the English to regroup and continue the fight. Another catastrophic error was made when the Scots moved down to meet the English forces from their strategic position on a hill after gaining initial early success in the battle. They found themselves in soft marshy ground which had not been visible from their previous position. The soldiers at the front of the Scottish army were trapped in knee high mud and many were killed as a result of being pushed over by the lines of soldiers behind them still advancing. It was also here in this boggy ground that the Scottish foot soldiers main weapon the "Pike" basically a sixteen foot long spear type weapon was found to be too cumbersome and unwieldy to use compared to the much shorter "Bill" a multi purpose weapon which the English soldiers preferred. The Scottish officers and commanders were also in the habit of leading from the front and again this was a fundamental mistake as they were killed or injured in the early stages of the conflict, leaving the Scots for the most part leaderless.

The outcome of the battle was that Scottish forces suffered what is probably their worst defeat in history with anything between ten and fifteen thousand men being killed, depending on which report you read. The English forces too must have suffered considerable losses because it seemed there was no attempt to take advantage of the situation and move into Scotland after the battle with the intention of possibly even capturing Edinburgh. The King of Scotland, the last British monarch to date to have been killed in action, plus a whole generation of administrators, thinkers, leaders, and vast numbers of Scottish nobility had been killed. They had been wiped out in less than an afternoon, and according to one report "there was not one family in Scotland who did not have a grave at Flodden" Such carnage would not be repeated thankfully until the horrors of trench warfare occurred during The First World War in France.

We are now well and truly on the last leg of our journey, but once again I am going to deviate off the route to visit Duns. Duns is a small town roughly ten miles North of Coldstream and well away from the Tweed, but Duns was the home of one of Scotland's motor racing legends Jim Clark.

Jim Clark was born in Fife in 1936 to a farming family and when he was very young, his parents moved to a farm near Duns. Jim Clark started his racing career in rallies and hill-climbs, totally against his parents wishes. He had a lot of early success in these types of races, but it was Boxing Day 1958 when he finished second in a race that was really the

start of his career. The man who beat him in that race was none other than Colin Chapman the founder of Lotus cars. Colin Chapman was so impressed with Jim Clark's driving ability that he offered him a drive in one of his Formula Junior cars. This was the start of a great partnership between Clark, Chapman and Lotus cars. Unfortunately Jim Clark's racing career was brought to a premature end when he was killed in a Formula Two race at Hockenheim Germany in 1968. At the time of his death he had achieved more grand prix wins, (25) and more grand prix pole positions (33) than any other driver. He is still, despite there being so many more races per season, the record holder for the highest percentage of laps in the lead in a season and also the record holder for Grand Slams achieved, that is, pole position, fastest lap, winning the race and leading every lap in the race. This was achieved in no less than eight grand prix races between 1962 and 1965. But it was not just Grand Prix driving where his ability showed, he had a sixth sense for cars and was able to drive and achieve results in virtually any vehicle.

He won the British Touring Car Championship in a Lotus Cortina. He drove in NASCAR in a Ford Galaxie for the Holman Moody team. Driving a Lotus Cortina he was a competitor in the 1966 RAC Rally of Great Britain and in 1959, 1960 and 1961 competed in the Le mans twenty four hour race in a Lotus Elite and an Aston Martin DBR1 gaining top three finishes. He also achieved success in the Indianapolis 500 where he led for 190 of the 200 laps with what was then an astonishing average speed of over 150 miles per hour and became the first non American for nearly half a century to win at the legendary Brickyard Circuit. Just to show his exceptional versatility he also competed in stock car racing in America driving a seven litre Holman Moody Ford on the banked circuit at Rockingham, North Carolina. There is a small museum dedicated to Jim Clark in Duns and the amount of trophies, cups and assorted silverware he managed to collect in only a few very short years, prove he was truly an exceptional driver. Motor racing fan or not if you are ever in the area with an hour or two to spare it is well worth a visit.

NORHAM CASTLE

CHAPTER 13

norham castle, union bridge, paxton house

We return to the banks of the Tweed and resume our downstream journey. We are now so close to Berwick-on-Tweed and the North Sea, you can almost taste and smell the salt in the air. There are still however several interesting places to visit before arriving at our final destination and as we travel downstream we arrive at Norham. The village of Norham itself is very pretty but its importance as far as our story is concerned is because Norham had one of the most heavily fortified defensive towers in the Borders. This tower was situated on a hill overlooking the River Tweed and standing guard over a vital ford across the river. Because of its situation and its proximity to Berwick-upon-Tweed, Norham Castle was the target of many attacks. It was besieged at least thirteen times, the longest of these being for nearly a year when it was attacked by Robert the Bruce. It is perhaps easy to understand therefore how it earned the reputation as being the most dangerous place in the United Kingdom to live.

In 1497 James IV of Scotland laid siege to the castle and he pounded the walls with his heavy artillery. Included in his battery of guns was a cannon called Mons Meg, reputedly the biggest calibre canon in existence at that time, having a barrel with a diameter of approximately twenty inches (510mm) and weighing in the region of six tons (7000kg). This canon had been given to King James II in 1457 by Phillip the Good, Duke of Burgundy

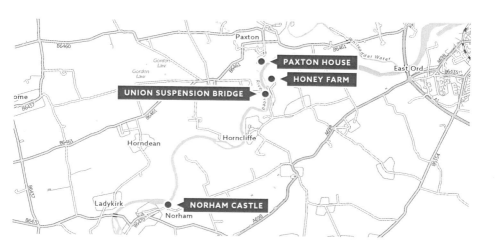

his uncle by marriage in order to help him "to interfere in English affairs" and it is thought to have been named after the area in which it was built in Belgium. This enormous cannon whilst very powerful and a formidable weapon was difficult to transport because of its weight and the generally poor condition of the roads. It required a team of horses to pull it and could only travel about three miles per day, a tremendous logistical operation in those times was required to even get it near a battle ground. The cannon would have to be positioned very carefully as once it was in position ready for firing, it could not be re-sited very easily. Mons Meg fired massive cannon balls. They weighed up to four hundred pounds each. These monstrous pieces of shot were up to ten times heavier than anything else in existence at that time and were able to inflict a considerable amount of damage to anything they hit. The canon though could only be fired about ten times a day due to the massive amount of heat produced by the huge charge of gunpowder necessary to propel the cannon balls towards their intended target which could be anything up to two miles away (over three kilometres). The siege at Norham Castle according to records was the only real conflict that Mons Meg was ever involved in and afterwards was only fired for ceremonial reasons, such as in the marriage of Mary Queen of Scots to Dauphin Francois in 1558. The cannon has now been fully restored and has pride of place on the battlements of Edinburgh Castle, where it is seen by thousands of visitors from all over the world every year.

I would like at this point in our story for you to pause for a minute to try and imagine that you are a young soldier on the ramparts of Norham Castle, the most dangerous place in Britain. You are standing on the castle walls some ninety feet above the ground, preparing to defend the castle against an approaching Scottish army. You don't really want to be there, you are a peasant farmer by profession, but like many of the others standing alongside you on the battlements you are required to help defend the castle in times of danger, this is part of the agreement which allows you to have the little piece of land which belongs to the castle and where you grow a few meagre crops in order that you and your family can survive. You have been called to arms by the local landowner to defend the castle when news of the invasion and forthcoming attack by the Scottish army was brought to the village. The Scots, still some distance away, have halted their advance, the tension is mounting, what will they do next? Suddenly there is a flash of light and a loud explosion, seconds later a huge canon ball, much bigger than anything fired previously, hits the castle walls, causing a huge amount of damage in the process. Can you even begin to think what thoughts might be going through his head, would the castle walls be able to withstand a prolonged bombardment from this new heavy weight cannon? What would be the outcome of the impending battle? Would his home be safe? Would his family sheltering in the castle be safe? No doubt though his main concern at that exact moment would probably be for his own safety. If the Scots managed to reach the castle and capture it, would they take prisoners or would everybody

NORHAM CASTLE

be slaughtered? Fortunately for him on this particular occasion the siege was brought to an early conclusion by the arrival of a hastily drawn together army of English reinforcements who arrived at Norham within a short space of time and were able to stop the Scots from advancing any further. Sixteen years later, the castle was once again attacked by James IV and this time he did in fact capture it. However his good fortune did not last and shortly after capturing Norham, he was killed and his army suffered a very heavy defeat at The Battle of Flodden in 1513 as described in previous chapters.

Norham Castle was perhaps one of, if not the strongest fortress in the Borders. With walls in certain parts being nearly nine metres thick, (that's approx. twenty eight feet thick.) There was a fortified building there from as early as 1121 and what made it easy to defend, but very hard to capture was its position and its structure. The castle is built on a mound on the South side of the River Tweed and its North face is protected by a steep slope leading down to the river. A deep ravine protects the East side and to complete its defences an artificial moat was dug on its South and West sides. The castle itself was built in two sections with an inner and outer section. The inner section was again built on a raised mound and was separated from the outer section by a moat which could only be crossed by a drawbridge. Having survived most of the attempts to capture it and having been rebuilt and repaired several times after these attacks, there was a period of relative calm in the Borders and by the end of the sixteenth century the castle was left to fall into disrepair. Norham Castle is now a Grade 1 listed building, in the care and control of English Heritage and it is open to the public.

We have rejoined the Tweed and after travelling only a short distance downstream, have arrived at The Union Suspension Bridge, which is less than six miles from Berwick. Work started on the building of this bridge in 1819 and it has a span of one hundred and thirty six metres or four hundred and forty nine feet. Building work was completed in 1820, at a cost of nearly six and a half thousand pounds. Because of the high cost of building, it was decided to make it a toll bridge and tolls for using the bridge were charged up until 1885. There was only one other similar style bridge in existence, the Menai Suspension Bridge which links the island of Anglesey with the Welsh mainland. Work to build the Menai Bridge had started sooner, but the Union Bridge being smaller was completed in a much quicker time and as a result it is classified as the oldest wrought iron suspension bridge in the world still carrying traffic, although traffic today is restricted by both size and weight and there are even discussions taking place regarding closing it completely because of the ever increasing costs of maintenance. The local inhabitants of the area were extremely happy that the bridge was built, they were even unconcerned at having to pay a toll when the bridge was opened as up until then it had meant either an eleven mile round trip downstream to Berwick or even worse a twenty mile round trip upstream to a place we have recently visited Coldstream, in order to cross the Tweed. In fact so popular was this particular crossing and due to the ever increasing amounts of traffic using it, another bridge was deemed necessary and this was built approximately sixty years later a little further upstream between Ladykirk and Norham.

THE BORDER UNION BRIDGE WITH PAXTON HOUSE IN THE BACKGROUND

Positioned only a short distance from the bridge is an independent, family owned business which has been in operation since 1948. This enterprise is known as The Chain Bridge Honey Farm and is open to the public. It has changed considerably in its sixty odd years of operation and now offers a huge range of honey based products from its on-site shop, including skincare products, moisturisers, soap, beeswax blocks, candles, and polish and of course not forgetting the honey itself, which is available either in jars as we generally buy it, or in cut comb sections. This is only a small selection of the items available and is well worth a visit, there are even lots of books available for those that might be interested in keeping a few bees themselves. The honey is produced from the business's own hives, over two thousand of them in fact and they are all situated within a forty mile radius of Berwick-on-Tweed. There is a working hive in the visitors area where you can see bees going about their daily business of making honey....don't worry its all behind protective screens so even youngsters can watch and marvel at what happens in a hive. In the grounds outside are a range of vintage vehicles, some of which have been restored and others are still in the process of being given loving care and attention. If seeing all the wonderful honey products and walking in the fresh air makes you hungry then there is always the opportunity to have a break at the café, which is situated on site in a vintage double decker bus of course, what else.

From the vicinity of the Honey Farm the roofs of a grand country house can be seen amongst the trees only a short distance away, this is Paxton House, less than four miles (seven kilometres) west of Berwick-on-Tweed and built on the North bank of the River Tweed, this means it is in Scotland but only just as the river at this point still acts as the Border, therefore it is only the gardens of Paxton and half the width of the river which distances it from England. The original house on the Paxton estate was owned by Margaret Home who had taken control after her husband died in 1744. Margaret had six children the eldest of whom was Patrick. After his fathers death Patrick had been sent to Leipzig to further his education and during his time there had become involved in the court of Frederick The Great and in particular with Sophie a Lady in Waiting to the Queen of Prussia. He then asked for and was granted permission to marry her by Frederick on condition that he stayed in Prussia. Patrick's mother was aghast at this idea and threatened to disinherit him if he agreed to Frederick's wishes. Not wishing to upset his mother or indeed lose his inheritance he then travelled through Europe and in particular Italy. Having spent some considerable time touring he was actually en-route to re-new his friendship with Sophie when he received word that his mother had been murdered by their butler. His travels were curtailed at that point and he returned to Scotland to take control of the family estate and attend the trial. Patrick had the idea of building a grand house at Paxton to try and tempt Sophie to come and live there and he had plans for the building drawn up by architect John Adam in 1757. Construction began in 1758 under the supervision of a Master Mason from Kelso called James Nisbet. By the time the building was finished in 1763 however it had become clear that Sophie was not interested in coming to Scotland and Patrick lost interest in the whole project.

In 1766 Patrick inherited Wedderburn Castle, an estate adjacent to Paxton and a few years later in 1771 decided to build a new house there. He then sold Paxton House to his cousin Ninian in 1773 for the princely sum of £15,000. Ninian had made considerable sums of money from his sugar plantations but wanted a base in Scotland where he could stay when he visited, he did not have the time to supervise the decorating or fitting out of the house and left it entirely to a company called Chippendale, Haig and Company. The result was that Paxton House now contains what is generally recognized as being the best collection of Chippendale furniture anywhere in the world. Unfortunately Ninian was killed in a slave uprising on his Grenada estates in 1795 and Paxton was then inherited by Ninian's younger brother George. In 1812 following the death of Patrick Home, George also inherited Wedderburn and it was he who decided to add another wing to Paxton house. Designed by architect Robert Reid, the extension was primarily needed to house the vast collection of books, paintings and furniture, collected by Patrick Home of Wedderburn during his Grand European Tour. George Home then devoted his life to cataloguing everything in the collection. The result of his labours are what you are able to see today, along with the gardens and grounds and various woodland walks.

Our journey along the River Tweed is now nearly complete and we are fast approaching our final port of call. I have not really touched on the subject of the food and hospitality which is available in the Borders, simply because there are so many good examples that it would take several pages to list them all and even then would not do them justice. Hotels, pubs, restaurants, bed and breakfast establishments, and cafes are all now catering for visitors from around the world as well as the local population. Whilst you will therefore still be able to enjoy a traditional fish and chip meal, you could just as easily be eating a Chinese, Indian, Thai, Japanese, Polish or Italian meal, especially in the bigger towns. Scotland generally is blessed with a natural larder which is full of high quality fruit, vegetables, fish, meat and game. Just the thought of a few well known dishes is enough to set my tastes buds into overdrive. Cullen Skink, a thick soup made with onions, potatoes and smoked haddock. Stovies, mainly potatoes and onions with the addition of left over meat, traditionally from the Sunday joint, but any left over meat can be used. For dessert a slice of Clootie Dumpling, currants, sultanas, flour, suet, golden syrup and spices wrapped in a cloth (Cloot) and left to simmer in a pot of boiling water for at least two hours. This piece of loveliness has of course to be accompanied with a liberal helping of custard. A meal fit for a King and I haven't even included delicacies such as haggis, black pudding, square sausage, tattie scones, porridge, shortbread, Selkirk bannock or Whisky.

The Scots as a nation are considered to have a sweet tooth and this is borne out by the fact that several of the Border towns have sweets or confectionery named after them such as Moffat Toffee, Hawick Balls, Soor Plooms (sour plums from Galashiels) Jethart Snails, and Berwick Cockles. I must also mention Edinburgh Rock and Tablet, but there I have to stop as I have a book to complete and all this talk of food does nothing to help my concentration.

BERWICK DEFENSIVE EMBANKMENTS

CHAPTER 14

berwick-on-Tweed

We have now arrived at Berwick-upon-Tweed, the most Northerly town in England. This dubious honour however, made it very vulnerable, being positioned only a few miles South of the Border. During the 17th and early 18th centuries if the words Berwick "Smack" were mentioned in your prescence it was not a warning that you were about to receive a blow to the head. Instead this was the name given to a type of cargo ship which was built in the immediate area. These vessels, had one central mast, which carried a vast amount of sail and were approximately seventy feet long and able to carry about 120 tons of cargo. They were used mainly between the ports of Berwick and London.

Carrying goods and indeed passengers by land was a slow and uncomfortable journey. Traveling by sea was cheaper and given favourable weather conditions, much quicker. The journey to London could be achieved in three days or less. The goods carried to the capital by the "Smacks" were grain, butter, eggs, pork and wool with huge amounts of North Sea herring and Tweed Salmon. There was even a very inventive and ingenious way of keeping the salmon fresh. This was achieved by having a well in the carcass of the ship into which fresh seawater could flow. The salmon were thus able to be transported alive and therefore in a much better condition on arrival in London. They were thus

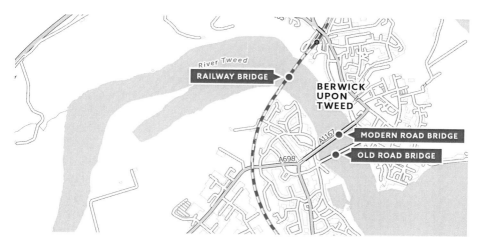

BERWICK EMBANKMENTS

able to command premium prices at Billingsgate fish market, as previously all fish had to be cured and smoked for the long and tedious journey to the capital. By the end of the 18th Century as many as twenty to thirty of these vessels could be seen in Berwick Harbour. Because of its fishing industry, international sea port, import and export trades and farming, and its position adjacent to the Border, the town was considered a rich prize and Berwick was attacked, captured, looted and ransacked at least thirteen times and probably changed hands a similar number of times before the end of the fifteenth century. Berwick is the only remaining Elizabethan walled town in England. The walls and earth embankments were built between 1558 and 1570, during the reign of Queen Elizabeth 1st of England. Defences up to this point in time, had relied on towers which, whilst giving defenders excellent views of their approaching attackers, meant they were obvious targets for enemy guns and with artillery becoming more accurate and powerful, they could quite easily be reduced to rubble. The new defences surrounding Berwick, were built by the well known military engineer Sir Richard Lee and loosely based on a design which was popular in Italy. The walls were thirty to forty feet high and featured Bastions, angular constructions projecting out from the main defensive wall, sited within gunshot range of each other, and built to the same height as the walls. There are five in total round Berwick's defensive walls. The embankments had stone cladding to approximately half their height, but they were mainly built from earth and rubble. This style of construction meant that even if cannonballs pierced the outer layer they lost all their force and effectiveness in the relatively soft earth. Troops and artillery in the

Bastions had all areas covered. With solid floors in the Bastions cannon could be quickly re-sited to cover danger areas. Attackers had nowhere to hide and could be caught in a devastating cross-fire. The building of these walls was a monumental task and considered to be the most expensive project of the Elizabethan era. The walls today are still very much in evidence and for the most part are intact and freely available to the public. A gentle stroll round the walls, can be completed in a little over an hour and is well worth the time, if only to enjoy the views across the Tweed Estuary. A gateway in the embankment leads you through to Berwick Barracks. The first purpose built accommodation for troops in Britain. The troops in Berwick had previously been billeted with local townspeople or in nearby inns. The cost of this was a heavy burden on the local community and complaints were made to the Government. The government of the period actually took notice of these complaints and possibly because they were still concerned that the Scots could be a problem, agreed to build living quarters for the troops. Captain Thomas Philips a military engineer, built the Barracks based on a design by well known architect Nicholas Hawksmoor. Work began on the Barracks in 1717 and the buildings were completed four years later in 1721. On completion they were able to house up to six hundred troops and thirty six officers. Berwick Barracks are now home to the Regimental Museum for the Kings Own Scottish Borderers. The regiment was formed in March 1689 by The Earl of Leven to defend Edinburgh against the Jacobite forces of James 2nd. The museum is open to the public and contains badges, relics, medals, weapons and uniforms from the various campaigns and battles in which the regiment took part. Due to financial cutbacks and defence reviews they merged in 2004 with The Royal Scots to form The Royal Scots Borderers. Then in 2006, further reviews took place and the name was changed to the 1st Battalion Royal Regiment of Scotland.

We have never been far away from bloodshed and violence during the course of our downstream journey, so it is perhaps fitting that towards the end of our travels we can relate a story where the exact opposite occurred. This happened in 1639 when the army of Charles 1st. met the army of General Alexander Leslie at Berwick. Although the armies were confronting each other, no fighting took place. Instead the commanders of the opposing forces met and discussions were held. A settlement was reached and "The Pacification of Berwick" was the resultant treaty. All this was put into place before a drop of blood could be spilt on either side. A good result all round for everybody concerned, I should imagine, and what a pity all disputes could not be settled in a similar fashion.

The Act of Union between England and Scotland in 1707 effectively ended confrontation between the two nations and Berwick was then officially declared to be English. There have been concerted efforts at various times to have Berwick returned to Scotland the latest being as recently as 2008. Amongst the topics under consideration

RIVER TWEED AT BERWICK

was actually moving the existing Scottish/English Border twenty miles South which would then incorporate Berwick into Scotland, however any such move would be a legal and logistical nightmare and has so far gone no further than being discussed. There is one aspect of Berwick however that does very much have, a Scottish connection, their football team, Berwick Rangers F. C. was formed in 1881 but despite being based in England they play in the Scottish Third Division. The reasoning behind this unusual situation is mainly geographical and means that the Berwick Rangers fans do not have to travel as far to away games as they would if they were playing in the English leagues. Berwick also has a Rugby Union team which similarly plays in the Scottish Leagues.

A frequent visitor to Berwick-on-Tweed from the mid 1930's until his death in 1976, was the artist L. S. Lowry. Famous for his paintings and drawings of industrial landscapes of Northern England and the human figures in his paintings which are often referred to as "matchstick men". Lowry was born in Stretford, Lancashire in 1887 and in his teenage years took private lessons in antique and freehand drawing. It was not however until the 1920's that he developed his own unique style. On his visits to Berwick, Lowry would stay at the Castle Hotel, in the centre of town. Because of his frequent visits to Berwick and his love for the town he was looking to buy a property, preferably on the embankment looking out towards the sea. Property records show however that no such purchase ever took place. There are approximately thirty drawings and sketches by Lowry, depicting street scenes and landscapes in and around the Berwick area. This collection has resulted in the "Berwick Lowry Trail" a walk, which allows you to follow in the footsteps of the artist to the various points where his paintings and sketches originated. Lowry also holds the dubious record for the most rejected British honours in his lifetime, including a knighthood which he was offered and which he refused in 1968.

There is one curious story which surfaces every now and then regarding Berwick-on- Tweed and is certainly a talking point, if only for the tourist industry of the town. The story goes that Berwick is still technically at war with Russia. It all stems from the fact that Berwick changed hands so many times in bygone eras that in any formal treaties or declarations, Berwick was added as a seperate name to the treaty as in "England, Scotland, and Berwick on Tweed." One of these declarations was the declaration of war against Russia during the Crimean crisis. However when the Treaty of Paris was signed in 1856 which officially ended the war, Berwick on Tweed's name was not there. In theory this meant that one of Great Britain's smallest towns was still at war with one of the worlds greatest superpowers. Nationwide, a B.B.C. television programme investigated this phenomenon and it was discovered that Berwick had not even been mentioned in the declaration of war either. The question then arose as to whether Berwick had actually been at war with Russia in the first place. The truth of the matter is however, that after

THE OLD BERWICK ROAD BRIDGE

THE ROYAL BORDER RAILWAY BRIDGE

The Wales and Berwick Act of 1746 any reference to England , would and did also include Berwick. There is an amusing little postscript to this story. It happened when the London Correspondent of Pravda, the international Russian newspaper, visited the Mayor of Berwick in December 1966. After discussing this curious situation they apparently decided to make a joint declaration of peace. The mayor of Berwick Councilor Robert Knox is reported to have said to the correspondent after their peace declaration, "Please tell the Russian people, through your newspaper that they can now sleep peacefully in their beds"

The River Tweed at Berwick is crossed by three bridges, all within a relatively short distance of each other. The most significant of these is surely The Royal Border Bridge built between 1847 and 1850. Despite its name it does not cross the Border, in fact the Border is some three miles further North. The bridge was designed by Robert Stephenson, whose father was George Stephenson and was originally built for The York, Newcastle and Berwick railway line. Even today it still carries the railway tracks which form part of the Main East Coast Line between London and Edinburgh. The bridge itself is more than six hundred metres long (over two thousand feet) and more than thirty six metres high (one hundred and twenty feet,) with twenty eight arches. It is indeed a very impressive structure. It was not until the 1990's that it needed any significant repair work, testament indeed to the engineer and builders who created it nearly one hundred and fifty years before. The Royal Border Bridge, however is not the oldest bridge in Berwick, that accolade goes to the nearby road bridge which is more than two hundred years older having been built between 1611 and 1624 and is now a Grade 1 listed structure. The construction of this bridge was ordered by James 1st of England (also King James 6th of Scotland) after he had travelled across the then rather rickety wooden bridge on route from Scotland to England for his coronation in 1603. The bridge was the main route across the River Tweed for travellers heading both North and South and it was not until the 1920's that a modern concrete bridge was built to carry the ever increasing volumes of traffic. In the 1980's however, a by-pass was constructed to the West of the town and this then carried the main road through Berwick, (the A1) and all the traffic that used it away from the town completely, much to the relief of the local residents who had previously had to suffer endless queues of cars and lorries trying to negotiate their way through the town's narrow streets.

We have now reached the end of our journey, some ninety seven miles from that little trickle of water coming out of a hole in the ground on a Scottish hillside. We have travelled through centuries of history, been enthralled by tales of Romans, Scots, French and English. We have heard about battles, wars, feuds, murders, blackmail and robbery We have visited vast estates and grand country houses, heard about building projects large and small, talked about various sports including rugby, fishing, golf, walking, motor sport and cycling. We have been introduced to many people, some have been famous and some have been infamous, but we have discovered their lifestyle and what it was like to live and work in the Borders in days gone past. Then there is the scenery, the rolling Border Hills, the forests, the woodlands, the moors and the river, always that river, sometimes in the background as part of another story, but more often than not the main player. Sometimes fast and turbulent, sometimes slow, dark and moody but always a part of what we have uncovered along the way. Now we are here in Berwick-on-Tweed, where the river flows far into the North Sea. Is this where the story ends? or will it just keep rolling along like the River Tweed itself.

ACKNOWLEDGEMENTS

Whilst this book has taken up a considerable amount of my time, which has involved collecting the information within it, putting that information together and visiting most of the places mentioned it has been thoroughly enjoyable and it certainly would not have been possible without the help of the people mentioned below to whom I owe an immense debt of gratitude.

My appreciation to William Bain, Dawyck Arboretum, Kailzie Gardens, Traquair House and Abbotsford for providing photographs.

However it is to Anne Denham and her husband John (friends from my schooldays) who on my behalf travelled the length and breadth of the Borders and not only provided the majority of photographs but put up with my endless queries and questions, despite leading very busy lives themselves... thank you.

There are many others, too many to mention who have also contributed, none more so than my wife Paula, who has had to endure months of solitude as I sat in front of a computer screen tapping away at the keyboard and who has probably been asked to read the script as often as I have read it myself, your help and understanding is much appreciated.

A final thank you, to you, because if you are reading this, you have purchased the book and I hope that it has led to a greater understanding of Borders life, culture and history whilst making your visit to The Borders even more enjoyable and that you will come back again and again.

Tweed Tales
A Journey Through The Scottish Borders

Copyright © Jim Collins 2016
jim.collinstweedtales@gmail.com

ISBN: 978-1-5262-0202-4

First published in 2015 by Jim Collins

Photographs:
© Jim Collins, pages 5, 7, 9, 24, 25, 39, 53, 59, 86, 87, 94, 99, 102, 104,107, 114, 116, 117. © Anne & John Denham, pages 20, 22, 42, 45, 60, 65, 71, 72,74,76, 81, 83, 85, 89, 91, 92, 95, 97, 109, 112, 119, 120, 121. © Royal Botanic Gardens Edinburgh, pages 17, 18. © Moira Leggat, Kailzie Gardens, pages 26, 28. © Traquair Charitable Trust, pages 31, 32. © William Bain, page 41. © Abbotsford House, pages 50, 51, 54, 55.

Design and layout:
Amy Bolt

Printed in the U.K by Emtone Print Ltd

All information in the book was correct at time of writing and that the author cannot be held responsible for changes or alterations which have occurred since.